Of the People,
by the People,
for the People

OF THE PEOPLE, BY THE PEOPLE, FOR THE PEOPLE

And Other Quotations by
ABRAHAM LINCOLN

Gabor S. Boritt
and
Jakob B. Boritt
Deborah R. Huso
Peter C. Vermilyea

Columbia University Press
New York

Columbia University Press
Publishers Since 1893
New York   Chichester, West Sussex
Copyright © 1996 Columbia University Press
All rights reserved

Library of Congress Cataloging-in-Publication Data
  Of the people, by the people, for the people, and other quotations
from Abraham Lincoln / [selected by] Gabor Boritt.
    p.   cm.
  Includes bibliographical references (p.   ).
  ISBN 0-231-10326-3 (alk. paper)
  1. Lincoln, Abraham, 1809–1865—Quotations. I. Boritt, G. S.,
1940–   . II. Title.
E457.99.H84   1996   96-31895
973.7'092—dc20   CIP

Casebound editions of Columbia University Press books are printed on
permanent and durable acid-free paper.
Printed in the United States of America
c 10 9 8 7 6 5 4 3 2 1

For Liz
Again
and
Always

Contents

*I*NTRODUCTION

By the time Abraham Lincoln's father, Thomas, grew old he could no longer sign his name. His mother, Nancy Hanks, never could. Their son took the road from the illiterate world of his parents to the Gettysburg Address and the Second Inaugural. What a road that was, what a distance to travel in a lifetime. The terrain covered may have been the most important in American history. This book attempts to chronicle faithfully those of Lincoln's travels that can serve us well in the twenty-first century.

* * * * *

Lincoln has been my friend since my late teens in South Dakota. Before that, in my childhood in Hungary, I knew almost nothing about the man. Landing in the United States I found him quickly, and he helped teach me English. I was a poor boy and a poor student, but Lincoln turned out to be a peerless teacher of the language. How grateful I am for that to this day. He taught me much besides English: about trying to be decent in difficult times, about rising in life, about democracy, friendship, strength, defeat, victory, and, above all, the virtue of common sense. Slowly, I read all that survived from his speeches and writings.

In time, I became a historian and Lincoln my subject. Though I never ceased to admire him, I had to learn to distance myself to be a scholar, to enter the guild of professional historians. That, too, was a satisfying experience. But now, after decades of work as a teacher and writer about Lincoln and his age, I again read every one of his words to create this book. The experience turned out to be remarkable, a rebirth of my early love. In my youth I had followed Emerson's advice and "hitched my wagon to a star," and now in middle age have found that I could be as star-struck as ever. While working on this book Lincoln became my close friend again and, as he said long ago, "the best part of one's life consists of his friendships."

Bookshelves bulge with "wits and wisdoms of Abe." Lincoln belongs to Everyman, and sometimes it seems that everyone puts words into his mouth, words people think he uttered or wish he had uttered. Not in this book. Every quotation here came from Lincoln's pen or mouth; most from longer letters or speeches, some from drafts, fragments, marginal notations, and even poems. When manuscripts of speeches did not survive, texts and notes taken down in shorthand by reporters and clerks, and at times checked by Lincoln, are used, though such material, as a rule, is less trustworthy than texts in Lincoln's own hand. A very few items in this book have not been published before in his collected works. A few passages, as well as three speeches, are reproduced in full. Words Lincoln had underlined are put in italics, but original paragraphing appears only in longer selections, and each quotation begins with a capital letter. Of course his habit of substituting dashes for periods is not followed. Letters and words obviously missing are inserted, but other editorial notes are bracketed. A few sentences or fragments appear more than once, for some very rare gems demanded to be heard in more than one context.

The sources of all the quotations are identified but not their derivations. Such a labor of love should be undertaken by a scholar more learned than I. The work will be daunting. Lincoln's most famous statement about *Government*, for example, can be traced back, via various intermediaries, to John Wycliffe's 1384 translation of the Good Book: "The Bible is for the Government of the People, by the People, and for the People." Perhaps it can be traced beyond.

We also know that Lincoln relied on folk wisdom and repeated sayings that went back centuries. He could warn the Illinois Central Railroad, his large corporate legal client, to take speedy action—so a recently discovered manuscript shows—for "A stitch in time may save nine. . . ." This book includes a few such comments, though clearly not original to Lincoln.

All the same, in some instances the standards of selection had to be higher than those of the canonical edition of Lincoln's works. For example, it is reasonably clear to me that he did not write his numerous Thanksgiving Proclamations; nor the letter to General James L. Wadsworth, or that to Mrs. Lydia Bixby (who was supposed to have lost five sons in the Union cause, but did not); nor most of the texts of his annual messages to Congress, though the parts he did write are freely quoted here.

Only four quotations do not meet the stringent selection standards and these are clearly identified under the headings *Lies, the People, Politics,* and *Ten Cannots Lincoln Did Not Write.* Three of the four exceptions include "quintessential" Lincoln statements that will never be separated from the Civil War president, such as: "You can fool some of the people all the time, all the people some of the time, but you cannot fool all the people all the time." We may never know for certain whether Lincoln ever uttered these words—most likely not—or the exact other phrases of this small group. As for the fourth of these selections, it is included as a warning against the most commonly quoted counterfeit, however unintentional a one, "The Ten Cannots." Over the years it seemed to appear most every place, from the *Congressional Record* to Ann Landers and a speech of President Ronald Reagan. The Reverend William J. H. Boetcker wrote these "Cannots" homilies early in the twentieth century and put authentic Lincoln quotations on the reverse side of his text. Later borrowers ascribed all to the greater of the two men.

To keep to the high ground of authentic Lincoln words—excepting the above four quotations—some captivating comments had to be excluded. In all my years I have known only one person with something like a "photographic memory," to use the colloquial. Unless the numerous people who ascribed statements to Lincoln possessed such unexcelled memories (from diarists to memoirists writing decades after his death), the words they wrote down—some, many, all—could not be Lincoln's. Surely, often the substance was not Lincoln's. *Of the People, By the People, For the People* is a book of *quotations*.

Still, I will not resist cheating a little—ten paragraphs' worth. Here are some of the favorites, all very Lincolnesque, some much more plausibly tied to him than others, but none of which had survived in unquestionably his words. On his ancestry: "I don't know who my grandfather was but I'm much more interested in what his grandson will do." Finding two of his sons squabbling about a pocket knife, Lincoln said to the older boy: "Oh, let him have the knife, Bob, to keep him quiet." Bob shot back: "No; it's my knife, and I need it to keep me quiet." Another time a neighbor came upon Lincoln with two wailing sons in tow. The neighbor asked: "Why, Mr. Lincoln, what's the matter with the boys?" "Just what's the matter with the whole world," came the reply, "I've got three walnuts, and each wants two."

The president talked much about God, as this book testifies, but we also have people remembering him quoting the prayer of the non-praying man lost in an awful thunderstorm: "Oh, Lord, if it is all the same to you, give us a little more light and a little less noise." People telling untruths fascinated the lawyer-politician, and folks remembered him telling the story of the man angry about being called a liar by a friend. "Why didn't you make him prove it?" "That's why I am so mad; he did!" Lincoln was reminded, too, of "a hotel-keeper down in St. Louis, who boasted that he never had a death in his hotel, for whenever a guest was dying in his house he carried him out to die in the street." And after a pompous military funeral Lincoln is supposed to have quipped: "If General—— had known how big a funeral he would have had, he would have died long ago."

We have a plethora of "broad" stories ascribed to Lincoln. Visiting a hospital during the war, a young woman asked a soldier where his wound was. The prone man blushed and stayed silent. Lincoln came to the rescue: "Ma'am the bullet that wounded him would not have wounded you." And the many preacher jokes. The sermon: "The Bible mentions no perfect woman, so plainly there has been none." A lady in the back stands up: "I know a perfect woman and I've heard of her every day for the past six years." "Who was she?" "My husband's first wife."

Defeated in the senatorial contest of 1858 and walking home on a dark rainy night, Lincoln stumbled, righted himself, and commented: "It's a slip not a fall." But when asked about the defeat he admitted, "I feel just like the boy who stubbed his toe, too badly hurt to laugh and too old to cry." When seeking the presidential nomination he explained: "Our policy is to give no offence." When elected, Lincoln went home to his wife with, "Mary, we are elected." To friends he explained: "Well, boys, your troubles are over now, but mine have just begun." He asked a visitor from the Volunteer State: "Does liberty still thrive in the mountains of Tennessee?" Hearing that President James Buchanan intended to abandon a federal fort in South Carolina, Lincoln burst out: "If that is true they ought to hang him!" Holding forts he thought was "good ground to live and to die by." "In a choice of evils, war may not always be the worst choice."

As Commander-in-Chief he dismissed an officer who complained that William T. Sherman (not yet the famed general) had threatened to shoot him. "Threatened to shoot you?" Lincoln asked. "Well if I were you . . . I would not trust him, for I believe he would do it." General George B. McClellan had "the slows" and the president thought "he would like to *borrow*" the army. As for the bragging of "Fighting Joe" Hooker: "The hen is the wisest of all animal creation because she never cackles until the egg is laid." After Gettysburg, when Robert E. Lee escaped with his battered army across the Potomac River, Lincoln told George Gordon Meade that his pursuit of the enemy reminded him of an "old woman trying to shoo her geese across a creek." And when the pious complained that Ulysses S. Grant drank, the president inquired: "Do you know what brand of whiskey Grant drinks? I'd like to send a barrel of it to all my generals." Oh memory. How inventive you can be.

At the fateful cabinet meeting where Lincoln announced his intention to issue an Emancipation Proclamation, he explained, or so a diarist present later recorded: "I made a promise to myself, and to my Maker. . . . I do not wish advice about the main matter—for that I have determined for myself." At another time he mused: "If I were to try to read, much less answer, all the attacks made on me, this shop might as well be closed for any other business. I do the very best I know how—the very best I can; and I mean to keep doing so until the end. If the end brings me out all right, what is said against me won't amount to anything. If the end brings me out wrong, ten angels swearing I was right would make no difference." He also explained: "I am never easy now, when I am handling a thought, till I have bounded it north, and bounded it south, and bounded it east and bounded it west." Painter Francis Carpenter, who spent six months at the White House and not long after wrote a book about the experience, also noted how the president had told him: "I am very sure that if I do not go away from here a wiser man, I shall go away a better man, for having learned what a very poor sort of man I am." And "most people are about as happy as they make up their mind to be."

Lincoln could get angry at people, including his wife. After she overspent the budget for refurbishing the dilapidated White House, so it was recalled, his voice went shrill: "It would stink in the nostrils of the American people to have it said that the President of the United States had approved a bill over-running an appropriation of $20,000 for *flub dubs* for this damned old house, when soldiers cannot have blankets." When a gentleman insisted on pleading for the endorsement of a business venture, Lincoln exploded: "Do you take the President of the United States to be a commission broker? . . . There is the door."

Then we have memory of the biting wit of a man from whom everyone seemed to want something. After Lincoln caught a mild version of smallpox he growled: "Now, I have something I can give to everybody." It was "a great relief to get away from Washington and the politicians," he explained. "But nothing touches the tired spot." In a lighter vein, when asked how he liked being president, he was reminded of the man being "ridden out of town on a rail, tarred and feathered." When asked how that felt, the reply came: "If it was not for the honor of the thing, he would much rather walk."

Clouds covered the capital as Lincoln delivered his second inaugural address. But when he finished the sun burst out. "It made my heart jump," he commented. Lincoln's oldest friend remembered hearing: "Die when I may I want it said of me by those who know me best . . . that I always plucked a thistle and planted a flower when I thought a flower would grow." On the day of his assassination he declared his unceasing optimism about the United States: "We shall prove in a very few years, that we are indeed the treasury of the world." And we have his everlasting love, words to his wife Mary at Ford's Theatre when she wondered what people might think about the two old people holding hands: "They won't think anything about it." How I wish to have all this, and more, in Lincoln's very own words. And I am looking forward to the work of my friend and fellow historian, Don E. Fehrenbacher, distinguished Lincoln scholar and Pulitzer Laureate, who is collecting and evaluating the degree of trustworthiness in such "quotations" that are really recollected words.

* * * * *

The criteria for making selections for this book included, in addition to authenticity and quality of thought, wit, and language, the usefulness to the people of the twenty-first century—this while attempting to avoid doing violence to Lincoln's own time and place. If we are to learn from him, we must forgive him (if that is necessary) for being a highly successful and utterly practical man of his times. "In this country one can scarcely be so poor but that, if he *will*, he *can* acquire sufficient education to get through the world respectably," said he in 1852. As a minimum the historian can add: exempting women, African-Americans, and American Indians. Yet, mental qualifiers notwithstanding, Lincoln's thoughts beg to be pondered.

The most difficult statements to include in this book mentioned race. Lincoln lived in an age when race baiting was common, and he, too, told what to us are tasteless jokes about black people—as he did about Irishmen and Dutch (meaning German) farmers, the two largest immigrant groups of his time. But in his speeches and policies he did not attack the new-comers; he welcomed them. And he opposed slavery from his earliest days.

In the 1850s as the antislavery crusade entered mainstream America, Lincoln rose to be one of its leaders. His opponents then attempted to shift the political argument from slavery, an issue on which they could not win, to that of race, an issue on which they thought they could not lose. The Democrats, led by Senator Stephen A. Douglas, also of Illinois, argued, at times in crude language, that Lincoln and the Republicans did not merely wish to stop the expansion of slavery, but wished to bring about the social and political equality of black people. Lincoln replied in kind, poking fun at his nemesis. He explained, "It was a false logic that assumed because a man did not want a negro woman for a slave, he must needs want her for a wife." Lincoln avowed that he desired no civil rights for black people, only their right to the fruit of their own labor. Had he not done so, we would never have heard of Abraham Lincoln.

Useful or not, a sampling of what will seem to us his worst can be found in this book under the heading of *Race Relations*. Readers would get a fuller picture by checking simultaneously such categories as *Slavery*, *Emancipation*, *Black People Degraded*, *Black Soldiers*, and the *Declaration of Independence*. On balance, what they will find are the words of a man who earned the nineteenth century sobriquet of "Great Emancipator."

Of course he was a man of his times, and he sports his contradictions. I hope readers will smile when they get to *Favors* and find Lincoln saying half-seriously in 1858, "But I shall not ask any favors at all," followed in 1859 by "I am never done asking for favors." He changed his mind, and on some important questions his thought developed. "I am not nor ever have been in favor of making voters or jurors of Negroes," he truthfully vowed in 1858— and so saved room for himself to lead the nation toward freedom for both blacks and whites. By 1864, however, he pleaded, in fact demanded, votes for some black people for "they would probably help, in some trying time to come, to keep the jewel of liberty within the family of freedom." Similarly, in 1848 he warned against amending the Constitution: "No slight occasion should tempt us to touch it." But in 1865 he fought for the amendment abolishing slavery, calling it "a King's cure for all the evils." Including Lincoln's worst in this book, together with his best, will perhaps help us as we face a new century and a new millennium, for they illustrate that the finest of humanity never stops growing.

Nothing exemplifies Lincoln's contradictory expressions better than his views on government debt. He began his career by enthusiastically favoring borrowing. Through 1840 he favored loans to support Illinois' public works and economic development. Then his state went bankrupt, and by 1843 Lincoln spoke of government debt as a "ruinous" device, "fearful to contemplate." In the Congress of 1848 he announced resolutely that "I would not borrow money. I am against an overwhelming, crushing system." But speaking to the Congress of 1864 as president, he took for granted that "Men readily perceive that they cannot be much oppressed by a debt which they owe to themselves." By then he was spending money on a war to save the United States—and what it stood for.

His contradictory statements suggest two points. First, however eloquent, wise, or witty, Lincoln was not a philosopher but a practical politician. And second, in history, context is all important. Some years ago Don Fehrenbacher told my students the following funny story to make the idea of context memorable. I have repeated the gist of it ever since.

An old farmer was giving his ponderous testimony in court when the opposing lawyer sharply interrupted:

"Now, Mr. Jones, *did you*, or *did you not* say after the accident that you were not hurt?"

"Well, your honor, it was like this. I was heading to market and hitched up to the cart old Sal, my mule. We got going . . ."

The opposing lawyer interrupted again. "Mr. Jones, we have no time for this. All we need is a yes or no answer. *Did you*, or *did you not* say after the accident that you were not hurt?"

The witness started again: "I hitched up my mule . . ." but was interrupted for the third time. The judge, however, decided to humor the old farmer:

"Let him finish the story."

So he started for the fourth time. "I hitched up my mule to go to market. We were traveling happily when, all of a sudden, I heard this terrible noise. A big automobile speeding from behind crashed into us. I was thrown into the ditch, the cart was destroyed, and my poor Sal, she was a bloody mess. Then this big man got out of the automobile, walked up to Sal and said: 'Good Lord, this mule is *hurt* something awful.' He whipped out a gun and shot her. Then he came to me and said: 'Are *you* hurt?'"

Context is all important. Yet here we have a book of quotations that excises short statements from longer texts. The book carries both the advantages and disadvantages of the genre. One of the most difficult problems in creating it was minimizing violence to context—whether in terms of a text or a larger historical circumstance. To paraphrase Lincoln, I attended to the matter as well as I knew how, which, God knows, was not very well.

Here is a small example. We have a fine sentence from correspondence he sent to General Grant in January of 1865: "Please read and answer this letter as though I was not President, but only a friend." Lincoln's well deserved reputation for humility seems to shine. Yet the above sentence is part of a presidential request for a staff appointment for his son, Robert, a recent Harvard graduate. Of course the young man received an appointment, as captain, and served for a few months in the relative safety of Grant's "official family." His desire to "see something of the war before it ends" was satisfied.

One might justify the president's action—more acceptable to his time than ours—as not merely the result of a natural instinct to protect one's child, but as defense of the state's interests. Mrs. Lincoln had suffered from deep depression after son Willie died of illness in 1862. Later she vehemently opposed Robert's going into the service. Lincoln, too, had been deeply affected by Willie's death, and also by his wife's depression. The country needed a fully competent chief executive with as few family distractions as possible. Keeping Robert safe thus served the country. Having said this, Lincoln's procurement of his son's appointment, while the sons of hundreds of thousands of others were dying, remains a shameful episode of his life. His letter to Grant could not be quoted in this book without explaining all this: that the humble request amounted to an embarrassing order. And so "Please read and answer this letter as though I was not President, but only a friend" had to be left out lest the explanation become ten times as long as the quote.

Context was central to the creation of this book. Nonetheless, if the reader suspects abuse, or finds the rare contradictions in Lincoln's words—for on the whole these are rare, the above examples notwithstanding—turning to the full texts of his writings may be in order. Indeed, it will be disappointing if many users and readers of this book will not feel the urge to read more of Lincoln.

All in all, the man from Illinois has a coherent outlook that *Of the People, By the People, For the People* displays to both his advantage and, one hopes, that of the readers. Lincoln's perspective on life is still very much worth observing and, perchance, absorbing. So much of what he said was wisdom for his time and all time. And he also could be very funny.

Within the alphabetically arranged categories, the quotations appear in chronological order, unless a different arrangement got to a truer Lincoln. Such an interference in chronology, though rare, as indeed the process of selecting the quotes as a whole, interposes the scholar between reader and subject. Yet it may not be too much to say that letting Lincoln speak as he pleased, without commentary, brings the reader closer to the quintessential man than can any history or biography.

Readers will surely go at this book in different ways and, perhaps, in different ways at different times. Some will use it as a reference work, as needed. Well enough. Some will look up Lincoln's words for the sheer pleasure of reading. Some may end up going through the whole book, bit by bit, and find in Lincoln a friend for the rest their lives.

Let me give a hand at starting the pleasure. Look up *Tom-Foolery*: "He said he was riding bass-ackwards on a jass-ack. . . ." Go on to Lincoln's objection to *Lying*: "A specious and fantastic arrangement of words by which a man can prove a horse chestnut to be a chestnut horse." Don't miss the unusual category of *Brief Comments*, including his angry grumble: "I am constantly pressed by those who scold before they think. . . ;" and his dismissive note about an office seeker who claimed descent from a famous—and famously impotent—Virginian: "A direct descendent of one who was never a father." See his *Refusals, Weather Forecasts, Husbands and Wives, the United States,*

Freedom, and *the American Dream.* "A house divided against itself cannot stand. . . ." "Four score and seven years ago . . . a new birth of freedom . . . government of the people, by the people, for the people. . . ." "With malice towards none. . . ." Find Lincoln's Farewell to Springfield: "Trusting in Him, who can go with me, and remain with you and be everywhere for good, let us confidently hope that all will yet be well. To His care commending you, as I hope in your prayers you will commend me, I bid you an affectionate farewell."

What a long road from the illiterate world of Thomas Lincoln and Nancy Hanks. We can tie words to subjects and years to make guideposts, but their music and message is boundless and timeless.

Gabor Boritt
Spring 1996
Farm by the Ford
Gettysburg

$\mathcal{A}$CKNOWLEDGMENTS

In expressing thanks for the help with a book that draws so fundamentally on a lifetime of study, a lifetime of friends would need to be mentioned. In order to avoid making the acknowledgments interminable, I will limit them to those who contributed to this volume.

The one exception will be Robert V. Bruce, Lincoln scholar, historian of labor and of science, biographer, winner of the Pulitzer Prize, my teacher at Boston University, and my friend. His love of the language has both cautioned and inspired me.

In the autumn of 1994 James Raimes, the Assistant Director of Columbia University Press, invited me to create this book. Though I was and am deeply engaged in a work on the Battle of Gettysburg, it did not take long to give in to temptation. After all, I have been collecting Lincoln quotes for much of my life. I am grateful for the opportunity to go to print at last.

I invited three young people to become assistant editors, to make their own selections, and to help with the winnowing and the editing. Jakob Bagge Boritt, Writing Seminars major at The Johns Hopkins University, class of 1998, my middle son, a man of eminent good sense and good humor, is the winner of national writing awards. Deborah R. Huso, my research assistant at Gettysburg College, History and English major, graduated in three years as the valedictorian of the class of 1996. Peter C. Vermilyea, a 1994 Gettysburg graduate, is one of the finest students of history I have had the pleasure to work with in my three decades of teaching. My expectation that this book would benefit from the infusion of young voices into the selection process was not disappointed.

The four of us pulled together more than 3,700 quotations. From this we cut the text down to about 750. I made the final decisions. The selections were entered into the computer and triple checked for accuracy by my youngest son Daniel Adam Wilson Boritt and three Gettysburg students: Paul J. Hutchinson, Benjamin C. Knuth, and Sandra Skordrud. They were assisted by still another Gettysburg stalwart, Jeffrey R. Scott. Page proofs were ready by Tracy Schaal, Marti Shaw, and Linda Marshall as well as the four editors. All were supervised by the excellent Tina Fair Grim and Marti

Shaw of the Gettysburg Civil War Institute. Marti, my secretary, also helped in more ways than can be counted.

To paraphrase Senator Paul Simon of Illinois, I hope Lincoln worked on them as much as they worked on Lincoln. I thank them all for their devoted hard labors.

When I started this project I got on the internet, and also sent out a mass mailing, asking for favorite quotations to be included in this book. I received an avalanche of replies, from the most distinguished scholars, including several Pulitzer and Lincoln Prize winners, down to people totally unknown to the public but who, through their replies, testified to their intimate knowledge of Lincoln's words. I was touched, for example, by a James M. McPherson, overwhelmed by public demands on him, taking the time needed to make thoughtful selections; or a Ronald D. Rietveld spending "the better part of the evenings" for several weeks making his choices. It seemed evident that this book project touched a nerve and people enjoyed participating in its making. I thank them all. They did help. I ask forgiveness for what is left out. I too have absent cadences singing in my ear.

I suspect that I may have been the first historian to enter Lincoln texts into the computer, in the 1970s at Harvard University. It is fitting then that *Of the People, By the People, For the People* made use of a concordance of all of Lincoln's words lent by the distinguished historian and bestselling Lincoln biographer, David Herbert Donald. Of course a concordance, however fine, is no substitute for a book of quotations. It would never lead one, for example, to Lincoln's reference to the *Navy* as "Uncle Sam's web-feet."

I also wish to thank Cullom Davis and associates at the Lincoln Legal Papers, Springfield, Illinois; Lloyd Ostendorff, Dayton, Ohio; Michael Musick of the National Archives, Washington, D.C.; and Paul Romaine and Sandra M. Skordrud of the Gilder Lehrman Collection, on deposit at the Morgan Library in New York, for sharing with me unpublished Lincoln materials.

I wish to acknowledge using in the Introduction revisions of two short passages from an article I wrote for the *Christian Science Monitor* in 1989, and from a Congressional testimony I gave in 1996.

As always, my final word of thanks goes to my family. Liz, my wife, and our three sons, Norse, Jake, and Daniel, were never far from my thoughts. The two younger boys ably worked on this book.

Here then is *Of the People, By the People, For the People*. As the author-subject of this book said in a very different context (speaking of the United States), "The fruit is before us. Look at it. Think of it. Look at it, in its aggregate grandeur . . .": Abraham Lincoln himself.

G.S.B.

*A*BRAHAM LINCOLN

1809–1865

Abraham Lincoln is my name
And with my pen I wrote the same
I wrote in both haste and speed
and left it here for fools to read

"Childhood Verse" [1824–1826], reprinted in *Collected Works of Abraham Lincoln*, v. 1, p. 1. Rutgers University Press (1953, 1990).

ACTION

I shall do *less* whenever I shall believe what I am doing hurts the cause, and I shall do *more* whenever I shall believe doing more will help the cause. I shall try to correct errors when shown to be errors; and I shall adopt new views so fast as they shall appear to be true views.

Letter to Horace Greeley, August 22, 1862, reprinted in *Collected Works of Abraham Lincoln*, v. 5, p. 388. Rutgers University Press (1953, 1990).

Breath alone kills no rebels.

Letter to Hannibal Hamlin, September 28, 1862, reprinted in *Collected Works of Abraham Lincoln*, v. 5, p. 444. Rutgers University Press (1953, 1990).

As our case is new, so we must think anew, and act anew.

"Annual Message to Congress," December 1, 1862, reprinted in *Collected Works of Abraham Lincoln*, v. 5, p. 537. Rutgers University Press (1953, 1990).

Practice proves more than theory. . . .

"Annual Message to Congress," December 1, 1862, reprinted in *Collected Works of Abraham Lincoln*, v. 5, p. 536. Rutgers University Press (1953, 1990).

"Do nothing at all, lest you do something wrong" is the sum of these positions. . . .

"Speech in United States House of Representatives on Internal Improvements," June 20, 1848, reprinted in *Collected Works of Abraham Lincoln*, v. 1, p. 481. Rutgers University Press (1953, 1990).

But you must act.

Letter to General George B. McClellan, April 9, 1862, reprinted in *Collected Works of Abraham Lincoln*, v. 5, p. 185. Rutgers University Press (1953, 1990).

ADVICE

I do not place what I am going to say on paper because I can say it any better in that way . . . were I to say it orally, before we part, most likely you would forget it at the very time when it might do you some good.

> Letter to Joshua F. Speed, [January 3, 1842?], reprinted in *Collected Works of Abraham Lincoln*, v. 1, p. 265. Rutgers University Press (1953, 1990).
>
> About marriage and courage.

I would say more if I could; but it seems I have said enough.

> Letter to Joshua F. Speed, February 3, 1842, reprinted in *Collected Works of Abraham Lincoln*, v. 1, p. 268. Rutgers University Press (1953, 1990).

For my own views, I have not offered, and do not now offer them as orders; and while I am glad to have them respectfully considered, I would blame you to follow them contrary to your own clear judgement—unless I should put them in the form of orders.

> Letter to General Don C. Buell, January 13, 1862, reprinted in *Collected Works of Abraham Lincoln*, v. 5, p. 98. Rutgers University Press (1953, 1990).

Quite possibly I was wrong both then and now; but . . . I cannot be entirely silent.

> Letter to General Joseph Hooker, June 16, 1863, reprinted in *Collected Works of Abraham Lincoln*, v. 6, p. 281. Rutgers University Press (1953, 1990).
>
> On military strategy.

AGREEMENT

Please see Gen. Halleck today; and if you can get him half agreed, I agree.

> Letter to Edwin M. Stanton, March 7, 1863, reprinted in *Collected Works of Abraham Lincoln*, v. 6, p. 127. Rutgers University Press (1953, 1990).

ALARM

He could not be so alarmed at what he is so sure will never happen.

> "Speech to the Springfield Scott Club," August 14, 26, 1852, reprinted in *Collected Works of Abraham Lincoln*, v. 2, p. 140. Rutgers University Press (1953, 1990).
>
> On the election of opposition's presidential candidate.

ALCOHOL AND ALCOHOLISM

[Abandoning drunks to their fate is] so repugnant to humanity, so uncharitable, so cold-blooded and feelingless, that it never did, nor ever can enlist the enthusiasm of a popular cause. We could not love the man who taught it—we could not hear him with patience. The heart could not throw open its portals to it.

"Temperance Address," February 22, 1842, reprinted in *Collected Works of Abraham Lincoln*, v. 1, p. 275. Rutgers University Press (1953, 1990).

The practice of drinking . . . is just as old as the world itself. . . . It commonly entered into the first draught of the infant, and the last draught of the dying man.

"Temperance Address," February 22, 1842, reprinted in *Collected Works of Abraham Lincoln*, v. 1, p. 274. Rutgers University Press (1953, 1990).

Many were greatly injured by it; but none seemed to think the injury arose from the *use* of a *bad thing*, but from the *abuse* of a *very good thing*.

"Temperance Address," February 22, 1842, reprinted in *Collected Works of Abraham Lincoln*, v. 1, p. 274. Rutgers University Press (1953, 1990).

In my judgment, such of us as have never fallen victims, have been spared more from the absence of appetite, than from any mental or moral superiority over those who have.

"Temperance Address," February 22, 1842, reprinted in *Collected Works of Abraham Lincoln*, v. 1, p. 278. Rutgers University Press (1953, 1990).

To have expected them [alcoholics] to do otherwise than as they did— to have expected them not to meet denunciation with denunciation, crimination with crimination, and anathema with anathema, was to expect a reversal of human nature. . . .

"Temperance Address," February 22, 1842, reprinted in *Collected Works of Abraham Lincoln*, v. 1, p. 273. Rutgers University Press (1953, 1990).

Even though unlearned in letters, for this task, none others are so well educated [as reformed alcoholics]. To fit them for this work, they have been taught in the true school. *They* have been in *that* gulf, from which they would teach others the means of escape.

"Temperance Address," February 22, 1842, reprinted in *Collected Works of Abraham Lincoln*, v. 1, p. 276. Rutgers University Press (1953, 1990).

That the disease exists, and that it is a very great one is agreed upon by all. The mode of cure is one about which there may be differences of opinion.

"Reply to Sons of Temperance," September 29, 1863, reprinted in *Collected Works of Abraham Lincoln*, v. 6, p. 487. Rutgers University Press (1953, 1990).

When the victory shall be complete—when there shall be neither a slave nor a drunkard on the earth.

"Temperance Address," February 22, 1842, reprinted in *Collected Works of Abraham Lincoln*, v. 1, p. 279. Rutgers University Press (1953, 1990).

ALTERCATION

I entertain no unkind feeling to you, and none of any sort upon the subject, except a sincere regret that I permitted myself to get into such an altercation.

Letter to William G. Anderson, October 31, 1840, reprinted in *Collected Works of Abraham Lincoln*, v. 1, p. 211. Rutgers University Press (1953, 1990).

AMBITION

Every man is said to have his peculiar ambition. Whether it be true or not, I can say for one that I have no other so great as that of being truly esteemed of my fellow men. . . .

"Communication to the People of Sangamo County," March 9, 1832, reprinted in *Collected Works of Abraham Lincoln*, v. 1, p. 8. Rutgers University Press (1953, 1990).

Many great and good men . . . would aspire to nothing beyond a seat in Congress, a gubernatorial or a presidential chair; *but such belong not to the family of the lion, or the tribe of the eagle,*[.] What! think you these places would satisfy an Alexander, a Caesar, or a Napoleon? Never!

"Lyceum Address," Springfield, Illinois, January 27, 1838, reprinted in *Collected Works of Abraham Lincoln*, v. 1, p. 114. Rutgers University Press (1953, 1990).

Twenty-two years ago Judge [Senator Stephen A.] Douglas and I first became acquainted. We were both young then; he a trifle younger than I. Even then, we were both ambitious; I, perhaps, quite as much so as he.

With *me*, the race of ambition has been a failure—a flat failure; with *him* it has been one of splendid success.

"Fragment on Stephen A. Douglas," [December, 1856?], reprinted in *Collected Works of Abraham Lincoln*, v. 2, p. 382. Rutgers University Press (1953, 1990).

I have never professed an indifference to the honors of official station; and were I to do so now, I should only make myself ridiculous.

"Fragment on the Struggle Against Slavery," [c. July 1858], reprinted in *Collected Works of Abraham Lincoln*, v. 2, p. 482. Rutgers University Press (1953, 1990).

The proudest ambition he could desire was to do something for the elevation of the condition of his fellow man.

"Reply to John Conness upon Presentation of a Cane," November 13, 1863, reprinted in *Collected Works of Abraham Lincoln*, v. 7, p. 13. Rutgers University Press (1953, 1990).

*A*MERICAN ANCESTORS

That people were few in numbers, and without resources, save only their own wise heads and stout hearts.

"Eulogy on Henry Clay," July 6, 1852, reprinted in *Collected Works of Abraham Lincoln*, v. 2, p. 121. Rutgers University Press (1953, 1990).

See also FOUNDERS OF THE UNITED STATES

*A*MERICAN DREAM

We stand at once the wonder and admiration of the whole world, and we must inquire what it is that has given us so much prosperity, and we shall understand that to give up that one thing, would be to give up all future prosperity. This cause is that every man can make himself.

"Speech at Kalamazoo, Michigan," August 27, 1856, reprinted in *Collected Works of Abraham Lincoln*, v. 2, p. 364. Rutgers University Press (1953, 1990).

We proposed to give *all* a chance; and we expected the weak to grow stronger, the ignorant, wiser; and all better, and happier together.

"Fragment on Slavery," [July 1, 1854?], reprinted in *Collected Works of Abraham Lincoln*, v. 2, p. 222. Rutgers University Press (1953, 1990).

There is no permanent class of hired laborers amongst us. Twenty-five years ago, I was a hired laborer. The hired laborer of yesterday, labors on his own account today; and will hire others to labor for him tomorrow. Advancement—improvement in condition—is the order of things in a society of equals.

"Fragment on Free Labor," [September 17, 1859?], reprinted in *Collected Works of Abraham Lincoln*, v. 3, p. 462. Rutgers University Press (1953, 1990).

See also LABOR

Free labor—the just and generous, and prosperous system, which opens the way for all—gives hope to all, and energy, and progress and improvement of condition to all.

"Address before the Wisconsin State Agricultural Society, Milwaukee, Wisconsin," September 30, 1859, reprinted in *Collected Works of Abraham Lincoln*, v. 3, p. 479. Rutgers University Press (1953, 1990).

I hold the value of life is to improve one's condition. Whatever is calculated to advance the condition of the honest, struggling, laboring man, so far as my judgment will enable me to judge of a correct thing, I am for that thing.

"Speech to Germans at Cincinnati, Ohio," February 12, 1861, reprinted in *Collected Works of Abraham Lincoln*, v. 4, p. 203. Rutgers University Press (1953, 1990).

I am exceedingly anxious that this Union, the Constitution, and the liberties of the people shall be perpetuated in accordance with the original idea for which that struggle [of the American Revolution] was made, and I shall be most happy indeed if I shall be an humble instrument in the hands of the Almighty, and of this, his almost chosen people, for perpetuating the object of that great struggle.

"Address to the New Jersey Senate at Trenton, New Jersey," February 21, 1861, reprinted in *Collected Works of Abraham Lincoln*, v. 4, p. 236. Rutgers University Press (1953, 1990).

[The] promise that in due time the weights should be lifted from the shoulders of all men, and that *all* should have an equal chance. . . . If this country cannot be saved without giving up that principle—I was about to say I would rather be assassinated. . . .

"Speech in Independence Hall," Philadelphia, Pennsylvania, February 22, 1861, reprinted in *Collected Works of Abraham Lincoln*, v. 4, p. 240. Rutgers University Press (1953, 1990).

You can better your condition, and so it may go on and on in one ceaseless round so long as man exists on the face of the earth!

"Speech at New Haven, Connecticut," March 6, 1860, reprinted in *Collected Works of Abraham Lincoln*, v. 4, p. 25. Rutgers University Press (1953, 1990).

Thanks to all. For the great republic—for the principle it lives by, and keeps alive—for man's vast future,—thanks to all.

Letter to James C. Conkling, August 26, 1863, reprinted in *Collected Works of Abraham Lincoln*, v. 6, p. 410. Rutgers University Press (1953, 1990).

AMERICAN INDIANS

I really am not capable of advising you whether, in the providence of the Great Spirit, who is the great Father of us all, it is best for you to maintain the habits and customs of your race, or adopt a new mode of life.

"Speech to Indians," March 27, 1863, reprinted in *Collected Works of Abraham Lincoln*, v. 6, p. 152. Rutgers University Press (1953, 1990).

ANGER

Unfortunately, however, it [your angry letter] reached Baker [Lincoln's friend] while he was writhing under a severe toothache, and therefore he, at that time, was incapable of exercising that patience and reflection which the case required.

Letter to William Butler, February 1, 1839, reprinted in *Collected Works of Abraham Lincoln*, v. 1, p. 141. Rutgers University Press (1953, 1990).

I understand my friend Kellogg is ill-natured—therefore I do not read his letter.

"Endorsement Concerning William Kellogg," [c. April 11, 1863], reprinted in *Collected Works of Abraham Lincoln*, v. 6, p. 167. Rutgers University Press (1953, 1990).

ANIMALS AND HUMANS

Beavers build houses; but they build them in nowise differently, or better now, than they did five thousand years ago. Ants, and honey bees, provide for winter; but just in the *same way* they did when Solomon referred the sluggard to them as patterns of prudence. Man is not the only animal who labors; but he is the only one who *improves* his workmanship.

"First Lecture on Discoveries and Inventions," [April 6, 1858], reprinted in *Collected Works of Abraham Lincoln*, v. 2, p. 437. Rutgers University Press (1953, 1990).

Climbing upon the back of an animal, and making it carry us, might not occur very readily. I think the back of the camel would never have suggested it.

"First Lecture on Discoveries and Inventions," [April 6, 1858], reprinted in *Collected Works of Abraham Lincoln* , v. 2, p. 440. Rutgers University Press (1953, 1990).

*A*NONYMOUS *AUTHORSHIP*

All I have to say is that the author is a *liar* and a *scoundrel*, and that if he will avow the authorship to me, I promise to give his proboscis a good wringing.

Letter To the People of Sangamon County, n.d., reprinted in *Collected Works of Abraham Lincoln*, v. 8, p. 429. Rutgers University Press (1953, 1990).

Reply to anonymous circular that claimed that Lincoln opposed paying an Illinois state debt.

*A*RGUMENTS

The President [James K. Polk] is nowise satisfied with his own positions. First he takes up one, and in attempting to argue us *into* it, he argues himself *out* of it.

"Speech in the United States House of Representatives: The War with Mexico," January 12, 1848, reprinted in *Collected Works of Abraham Lincoln*, v. 1, p. 441. Rutgers University Press (1953, 1990).

Has it not got down as thin as the homeopathic soup that was made by boiling the shadow of a pigeon that had starved to death?

"Sixth Debate with Stephen A. Douglas, at Quincy, Illinois," October 13, 1858, reprinted in *Collected Works of Abraham Lincoln*, v. 3, p. 279. Rutgers University Press (1953, 1990).

Senator Douglas' argument about popular sovereignty. See also POPULAR SOVEREIGNTY

One would start with great confidence that he could convince any sane child that the simpler propositions of Euclid are true; but, nevertheless, he would fail, utterly, with one who should deny the definitions and axioms.

Letter to Henry L. Pierce and Others, April 6, 1859, reprinted in *Collected Works of Abraham Lincoln*, v. 3, p. 375. Rutgers University Press (1953, 1990).

That makes an issue; and the burden of proof is upon you.

"Speech at New Haven, Connecticut," March 5, 1860, reprinted in *Collected Works of Abraham Lincoln*, v. 4, p. 26. Rutgers University Press (1953, 1990).

I do not argue. I beseech you to make the arguments for yourselves. You can not, if you would, be blind to the signs of the times.

"Proclamation Revoking General Hunter's Order of Military Emancipation of May 9, 1862," May 19, 1862, reprinted in *Collected Works of Abraham Lincoln*, v. 5, p. 223. Rutgers University Press (1953, 1990).

Call for voluntary emancipation by border states.

If there ever could be a proper time for mere catch arguments, that time surely is not now. In times like the present [Civil War], men should utter nothing for which they would not willingly be responsible through time and in eternity.

"Annual Message to Congress," December 1, 1862, reprinted in *Collected Works of Abraham Lincoln*, v. 5, p. 535. Rutgers University Press (1953, 1990).

*A*UTOGRAPHS

Your note, requesting my "signature with a sentiment," was received, and should have been answered long since, but that it was mislaid. I am not a very sentimental man; and the best sentiment I can think of is, that if you collect the signatures of all persons who are no less distinguished than I, you will have a very undistinguishing mass of names.

Letter to C.U. Schlater, January 5, 1849, reprinted in *Collected Works of Abraham Lincoln*, v. 2, p. 19. Rutgers University Press (1953, 1990).

*A*XES

An ax, or a miracle, was indispensable.

"First Lecture on Discoveries and Inventions," [April 6, 1858], reprinted in *Collected Works of Abraham Lincoln*, v. 2, p. 438. Rutgers University Press (1953, 1990).

On building an ark in the Bible.

*B*ANKS

In all candor, let me ask, was such a system for benefiting the few at the expense of the many ever before devised?

"Speech on the Sub-Treasury," December [26], 1839, reprinted in *Collected Works of Abraham Lincoln*, v. 1, p. 162. Rutgers University Press (1953, 1990).

On an alternative to a central bank.

If there is any one subject of which the people are more easily excited than any other—and in regard to which their jealousy never slumbers, it is as to the privileges and powers of Banks[,] therefore every precaution should be used by those institutions. . . .

"Committee Report in the Illinois Legislature on Condition of the State Bank," [January 21,1840], reprinted in *Collected Works of Abraham Lincoln*, v. 1, p. 191. Rutgers University Press (1953, 1990).

This [economic problem] is not attributable to any organic defects of the institutions themselves but to the irresistible law of trade and exchange which cannot be controlled by country banks.

"Committee Report in the Illinois Legislature on Condition of the State Bank," [January 21, 1840], reprinted in *Collected Works of Abraham Lincoln*, v. 1, p. 194. Rutgers University Press (1953, 1990).

See also MONEY

*B*ANKRUPTCY

It was just as bad to be bankrupt in one respect as in the other. . . .

"Remarks in Illinois Legislature," December 11, 1840, reprinted in *Collected Works of Abraham Lincoln*, v. 1, p. 219. Rutgers University Press (1953, 1990).

*B*EARD

As to the whiskers, having never worn any, do you not think people would call it a piece of silly affection if I were to begin it now?

Letter to Grace Bedell, October 19, 1860, reprinted in *Collected Works of Abraham Lincoln*, v. 4, p. 129. Rutgers University Press (1953, 1990)

After an eight-year-old suggested he grow a beard.

*B*IBLE, THE

I doubt not that it is really . . . the best cure for the "Blues" could one but take it according to the truth.

Letter to Mary Speed, September 27, 1841, reprinted in *Collected Works of Abraham Lincoln*, v. 1, p. 261. Rutgers University Press (1953, 1990).

The best gift God has given to man.

"Reply to Loyal Colored People of Baltimore upon Presentation of a Bible," September 7, 1864, reprinted in *Collected Works of Abraham Lincoln*, v. 7, p. 542. Rutgers University Press (1953, 1990).

*B*LACK PEOPLE DEGRADED

One after another they have closed the heavy iron doors upon him, and now they have him, as it were, bolted in with a lock of a hundred keys, which can never be unlocked without the concurrence of every key; the keys in the hands of a hundred different men, and they scattered to a hundred different and distant places. . . .

"Speech at Springfield, Illinois," June 26, 1857, reprinted in *Collected Works of Abraham Lincoln*, v. 2, p. 404. Rutgers University Press (1953, 1990).

Now, when by all these means you have succeeded in dehumanizing the negro; when you have put him down, and made it forever impossible for him to be but as the beasts of the field; when you have extinguished his soul, and placed him where the ray of hope is blown out in darkness like that which broods over the spirits of the damned; are you quite sure the demon which you have roused *will not turn and rend you?*

"Speech at Edwardsville, Illinois," September 11, 1858, reprinted in *Collected Works of Abraham Lincoln*, v. 3, p. 95. Rutgers University Press (1953, 1990).

You have taken the negro out of the catalogue of man. . . .

"Speech at Indianapolis, Indiana," September 19, 1859, reprinted in *Collected Works of Abraham Lincoln*, v. 3, p. 469. Rutgers University Press (1953, 1990).

*B*LACK SOLDIERS

The bare sight of fifty thousand armed, and drilled black soldiers on the banks of the Mississippi, would end the rebellion at once.

Letter to Andrew Johnson, March 26, 1863, reprinted in *Collected Works of Abraham Lincoln*, v. 6, p. 149. Rutgers University Press (1953, 1990).

To sell or enslave any captured person, on account of his color, and for no offense against the laws of war, is a relapse into barbarism and a crime against the civilization of the age. . . . It is therefore ordered that for every soldier of the United States killed in violation of the laws of war, a rebel soldier shall be executed; and for every one enslaved by the enemy or sold into slavery, a rebel soldier shall be placed at hard labor on the public works and continued at such labor until the other shall be released and receive the treatment due to a prisoner of war.

"Order of Retaliation," July 30, 1863, reprinted in *Collected Works of Abraham Lincoln*, v. 6, p. 357. Rutgers University Press (1953, 1990).

Reply to Confederate order to enslave captured black soldiers of the Union.

And then, there will be some black men who can remember that, with silent tongue, and clenched teeth, and steady eye, and well-poised bayonet, they have helped mankind on to this great consummation; while, I fear, there will be some white ones, unable to forget that, with malignant heart, and deceitful speech, they have strove to hinder it.

Letter to James C. Conkling, August 26, 1863, reprinted in *Collected Works of Abraham Lincoln*, v. 6, p. 410. Rutgers University Press (1953, 1990).

So far as tested, it is difficult to say they are not as good soldiers as any.

"Annual Message to Congress," December 8, 1863, reprinted in *Collected Works of Abraham Lincoln*, v. 7, p. 50. Rutgers University Press (1953, 1990).

Thus we have the new reckoning.

"Annual Message to Congress," December 8, 1863, reprinted in *Collected Works of Abraham Lincoln*, v. 7, p. 50. Rutgers University Press (1953, 1990).

Widows and children *in fact,* of colored soldiers who fall in our service, [must] be placed in law, the same as if their marriages were legal, so that they can have the benefit of the provisions made the widows and orphans of white soldiers.

Letter to Charles Sumner, May 19, 1864, reprinted in *Collected Works of Abraham Lincoln, Supplement 1832–1865*, v. 10, p. 243. Rutgers University Press (1953, 1990).

Keep it [black soldiers], and you can save the Union. Throw it away, and the Union goes with it.

Letter to Isaac M. Schermerhorn, September 12, 1864, reprinted in *Collected Works of Abraham Lincoln*, v. 8, p. 2. Rutgers University Press (1953, 1990).

Complaint is made to me that you are forcing negroes into the military service, and even torturing them—riding them on rails and the like—to extort their consent. I hope this may be a mistake. The like must not be done by you, or any one under you. You must not force negroes any more than white men.

Letter to John Glenn, February 7, 1865, reprinted in *Collected Works of Abraham Lincoln*, v. 8, p. 266. Rutgers University Press (1953, 1990).

*B*LACK SOLDIERS AS CONFEDERATES

If he shall now really fight to keep himself a slave, it will be a far better argument why [he] should remain a slave than I have ever before heard. He, perhaps, ought to be a slave, if he desires it ardently enough to fight for it. Or, if one out of four will, for his own freedom, fight to keep the other three in slavery, he ought to be a slave for his selfish meanness.

"Speech to One Hundred Fortieth Indiana Regiment," March 17, 1865, reprinted in *Collected Works of Abraham Lincoln*, v. 8, p. 361. Rutgers University Press (1953, 1990).

*B*LAME

I surely will not blame them for not doing what I should not know how to do myself.

"Speech at Peoria, Illinois," October 16, 1854, reprinted in *Collected Works of Abraham Lincoln*, v. 2, p. 255. Rutgers University Press (1953, 1990).

On how to deal with slavery.

I certainly know that if the war fails, the administration fails, and that I *will* be blamed for it, whether I deserve it or not. And I ought to be blamed, if I could do better. You think I could do better; therefore you blame me already. I think I could not do better; therefore I blame you for blaming me.

Letter to Carl Schurz, November 24, 1862, reprinted in *Collected Works of Abraham Lincoln*, v. 5, p. 509. Rutgers University Press (1953, 1990).

So ready are we all to cry out, and ascribe motives, when our own toes are pinched.

> Letter to General William S. Rosecrans, March 17, 1863, reprinted in *Collected Works of Abraham Lincoln*, v. 6, p. 139. Rutgers University Press (1953, 1990).

*B*OMBAST

Bombastic and hollow as Napoleon's bulletins sent back from his campaign in Russia.

> Letter to Gustave P. Koerner, July 15, 1858, reprinted in *Collected Works of Abraham Lincoln*, v. 2, p. 502. Rutgers University Press (1953, 1990).

*B*RIEF *COMMENTS*

Are you possessing houses and lands, and oxen and asses, and men-servants and maid-servants, and begetting sons and daughters?

> Letter to Joshua F. Speed, May 18, 1843, reprinted in *Collected Works of Abraham Lincoln*, v. 1, p. 325. Rutgers University Press (1953, 1990).

He is a good hand to raise a breeze.

> Letter to Elihu B. Washburne, April 30, 1848, reprinted in *Collected Works of Abraham Lincoln*, v. 1, p. 467. Rutgers University Press (1953, 1990).
>
> Describing politician Edward D. Baker.

But, what's in the wind?

> Editorial on the Right of Foreigners to Vote, July 23, 1856, reprinted in *Collected Works of Abraham Lincoln*, v. 2, p. 356. Rutgers University Press (1953, 1990).

It is to be dished up in as many varieties as a French cook can produce soups from potatoes.

> "Speech at Springfield, Illinois," July 17, 1858, reprinted in *Collected Works of Abraham Lincoln*, v. 2, p. 507. Rutgers University Press (1953, 1990).
>
> On the democratic platform.

There is much he can not do, and *some* he can.

> Letter to Joseph Gillespie, July 25, 1858, reprinted in *Collected Works of Abraham Lincoln*, v. 2, p. 523. Rutgers University Press (1953, 1990).
>
> On Illinois Senator Lyman Trumbull.

Some things are passing strange.

Letter to Gustave P. Koerner, August 6, 1858, reprinted in *Collected Works of Abraham Lincoln*, v. 2, p. 537. Rutgers University Press (1953, 1990).

Referring to false newspaper reports.

Can any mortal man misunderstand this language?

Fragment: "Notes for Speeches," September 15, 1858, reprinted in *Collected Works of Abraham Lincoln*, v. 3, p. 99. Rutgers University Press (1953, 1990).

Like causes produce like effects.

"Third Debate with Stephen A. Douglas at Jonesboro, Illinois," September 15, 1858, reprinted in *Collected Works of Abraham Lincoln*, v. 3, p. 121. Rutgers University Press (1953, 1990).

He contented himself with sneering. . . .

"Fifth Debate with Stephen A. Douglas at Galesburg, Illinois," October 7, 1858, reprinted in *Collected Works of Abraham Lincoln*, v. 3, p. 230. Rutgers University Press (1953, 1990).

Comes very near kicking his own fat into the fire. . . .

"Speech at Columbus, Ohio," September 16, 1859, reprinted in *Collected Works of Abraham Lincoln*, v. 3, p. 411. Rutgers University Press (1953, 1990).

On Senator Douglas.

Onward and upward. . . .

"Address before the Wisconsin State Agricultural Society," Milwaukee, Wisconsin, September 30, 1859, reprinted in *Collected Works of Abraham Lincoln*, v. 3, p. 482. Rutgers University Press (1953, 1990).

We shall try to do our duty.

"Speech at Leavenworth, Kansas," December 3, 1859, reprinted in *Collected Works of Abraham Lincoln*, v. 3, p. 502. Rutgers University Press (1953, 1990).

A question which the country will not allow me to evade.

Letter to General George B. McClellan, April 9, 1862, reprinted in *Collected Works of Abraham Lincoln*, v. 5, p. 184. Rutgers University Press (1953, 1990).

On leaving Washington undefended.

It seems the game is before you.

Letter to John C. Fremont, May 30, 1862, reprinted in *Collected Works of Abraham Lincoln*, v. 5, p. 251. Rutgers University Press (1953, 1990).

On the enemy.

You perceive I treat you no worse than I do others.

Letter to Isaac Pomeroy, March 3, 1860, reprinted in *Collected Works of Abraham Lincoln*, v. 3, p. 554. Rutgers University Press (1953, 1990).

Profoundly laid by.

Memorandum, [c. June 2, 1862], reprinted in *Collected Works of Abraham Lincoln*, v. 5, p. 257. Rutgers University Press (1953, 1990).

Marginal comment on 40 page legalistic memo suggesting that the U.S. go to war with France.

I think we better take while we can get.

Letter to Edwin M. Stanton, August 9, 1862, reprinted in *Collected Works of Abraham Lincoln*, v. 5, p. 365. Rutgers University Press (1953, 1990).

On soldiers offered to government.

Reconcile, as far as possible, all existing interests. . . .

"Annual Message to Congress," December 1, 1862, reprinted in *Collected Works of Abraham Lincoln*, v. 5, p. 523. Rutgers University Press (1953, 1990).

I may not be the most competent judge. . . .

Letter to Charles P. Kirkland, December 7, 1862, reprinted in *Collected Works of Abraham Lincoln*, v. 5, p. 544. Rutgers University Press (1953, 1990).

Righteous peace. . . .

Letter to Caleb Russell and Sallie A. Fenton, January 5, 1863, reprinted in *Collected Works of Abraham Lincoln*, v. 6, p. 39. Rutgers University Press (1953, 1990).

It won't do. Must have a tip-top man there next time.

Letter to William H. Seward, January 21, 1863, reprinted in *Collected Works of Abraham Lincoln*, v. 6, p. 69. Rutgers University Press (1953, 1990).

On diplomatic appointment.

Only those generals who gain successes, can set up dictators.

Letter to Joseph Hooker, January 26, 1863, reprinted in *Collected Works of Abraham Lincoln*, v. 6, p. 78. Rutgers University Press (1953, 1990).

A direct descendant of one who never was a father.

Memorandum: Appointment of Edgar Harriott, [c. February 17, 1863], reprinted in *Collected Works of Abraham Lincoln*, v. 6, p. 107. Rutgers University Press (1953, 1990).

On person claiming descent from John Randolph of Roanoke.

I am constantly pressed by those who *scold* before they *think*. . . .

Letter to John A. McClernand, August 12, 1863, reprinted in *Collected Works of Abraham Lincoln*, v. 6, p. 383. Rutgers University Press (1953, 1990).

Errors will occur in spite of the utmost fidelity.

"Opinion on the Draft," September 14 [?], 1863, reprinted in *Collected Works of Abraham Lincoln*, v. 6, p. 449. Rutgers University Press (1953, 1990).

Be of good cheer.

Letter to William S. Rosecrans. September 21, 1863, reprinted in *Collected Works of Abraham Lincoln*, v. 6, p. 472. Rutgers University Press (1953, 1990).

I exhausted my wits, and very nearly my patience. . . .

Letter to Charles D. Drake and Others, October 5, 1863, reprinted in *Collected Works of Abraham Lincoln*, v. 6, p. 502. Rutgers University Press (1953, 1990).

On dealing with infighting among Missouri Unionists.

Build only from the sound. . . .

"Annual Message to Congress," December 8, 1863, reprinted in *Collected Works of Abraham Lincoln*, v. 7, p. 51. Rutgers University Press (1953, 1990).

*B*ROWN, *JOHN*

Old John Brown has just been executed for treason against a state. We cannot object, even though he agreed with us in thinking slavery wrong. That cannot excuse violence, bloodshed, and treason. It could avail him nothing that he might think himself right.

"Speech at Leavenworth, Kansas," December 3, 1859, reprinted in *Collected Works of Abraham Lincoln*, v. 3, p. 502. Rutgers University Press (1953, 1990).

*C*APITAL

That men who are industrious, and sober, and honest in the pursuit of their own interests should after a while accumulate capital, and after that should be allowed to enjoy it in peace, and also if they should choose when they have accumulated it to use it to save themselves from actual labor and hire other people to labor for them is right.

"Speech at Cincinnati, Ohio," September 17, 1859, reprinted in *Collected Works of Abraham Lincoln*, v. 3, p. 459. Rutgers University Press (1953, 1990).

While we do not propose any war upon capital, we do wish to allow the humblest man an equal chance to get rich with everybody else.

"Speech at New Haven, Connecticut," March 5, 1860, reprinted in *Collected Works of Abraham Lincoln*, v. 4, p. 24. Rutgers University Press (1953, 1990).

See also LABOR

CEREMONIES

Please let ceremonies be only such as to take the least time possible.

Letter to Edwin D. Morgan, February 4, 1861, reprinted in *Collected Works of Abraham Lincoln*, v. 4, p. 185. Rutgers University Press (1953, 1990).

CERTAINTY

Just as sure . . . as tomorrow is to come. . . .

"Fifth Debate with Stephen A. Douglas at Galesburg, Illinois," October 7, 1858, reprinted in *Collected Works of Abraham Lincoln*, v. 3, p. 232. Rutgers University Press (1953, 1990).

CHANGE

The change it contemplates would come as gently as the dews of heaven, not rendering or wrecking anything. Will you not embrace it?

"Proclamation Revoking General Hunter's Order of Military Emancipation", May 19, 1862, reprinted in *Collected Works of Abraham Lincoln*, v. 5, p. 223. Rutgers University Press (1953, 1990).

On emancipation.

Believing as I do, that *gradual* can be made better than *immediate* for both black and white. . . .

Letter to John M. Schofield, June 22, 1863, reprinted in *Collected Works of Abraham Lincoln*, v. 6, p. 291. Rutgers University Press (1953, 1990).

On emancipation.

CHARACTER

Many eloquent men fail utterly; and they are not, as a class, generally successful. His judgment was excellent; but many men of good judgment live and die unnoticed. His will was indomitable; but this quality often secures to its owner nothing better than a character for useless obstinacy. These then were Mr. Clay's leading qualities. No one of them is very uncommon; but all taken together are rarely combined in a single individual; and this is probably the reason why such men as Henry Clay are so rare in the world.

"Eulogy on Henry Clay," July 6, 1852, reprinted in *Collected Works of Abraham Lincoln*, v. 2, p. 125. Rutgers University Press (1953, 1990).

The man for a crisis.

"Eulogy on Henry Clay," July 6, 1852, reprinted in *Collected Works of Abraham Lincoln*, v. 2, p. 129. Rutgers University Press (1953, 1990).

CHURCH AND STATE

The U.S. government must not undertake to run the churches.

"Note on petition of Second Presbyterian Church, Memphis," March 4, 1864, manuscript in Morgan Library, New York, Gilder Lehrman Collection, no. 4813.

CIVIL LIBERTIES

The cause of civil liberty must not be surrendered at the end of *one*, or even, one *hundred* defeats.

Letter to Henry Asbury, November 19, 1858, reprinted in *Collected Works of Abraham Lincoln*, v. 3, p. 339. Rutgers University Press (1953, 1990).

Must a government, of necessity, be too *strong* for the liberties of its own people, or too *weak* to maintain its own existence?

"Message to Congress in Special Session," July 4, 1861, reprinted in *Collected Works of Abraham Lincoln*, v. 4, p. 426. Rutgers University Press (1953, 1990).

If a commanding General finds a necessity to seize the farm of a private owner, for a pasture, an encampment, or a fortification, he has the right to do so, and to hold it, as long as the necessity lasts; and this is within military law, because within military necessity. But to say the farm shall no longer belong to the owner, or his heirs forever; and this as well when the farm is not needed for military purposes as when it is, is purely political, without the savor of military law about it. . . . It assumes that the general may do *anything.* . . .

Letter to Orville H. Browning, September 22, 1861, reprinted in *Collected Works of Abraham Lincoln*, v. 4, p. 531. Rutgers University Press (1953, 1990).

I have been unwilling to go beyond the pressure of necessity in the unusual exercise of power.

"Annual Message to Congress," December 3, 1861, reprinted in *Collected Works of Abraham Lincoln*, v. 5, p. 43. Rutgers University Press.

Let your military measures be strong enough to repel the invader and keep the peace, and not so strong as to unnecessarily harass and persecute the people. It is a difficult *role.* . . .

Letter to John M. Schofield, May 27, 1863, reprinted in *Collected Works of Abraham Lincoln*, v. 6, p. 234. Rutgers University Press (1953, 1990).

I can no more be persuaded that the government can constitutionally take no strong measure in time of rebellion, because it can be shown that the same could not be lawfully taken in time of peace, than I can be persuaded that a particular drug is not good medicine for a sick man, because it can be shown to not be good food for a well one.

Letter to Erastus Corning and Others, June 12, 1863, reprinted in *Collected Works of Abraham Lincoln*, v. 6, p. 267. Rutgers University Press (1953, 1990).

Nor am I able to appreciate the danger . . . that the American people will, by means of military arrests during the rebellion, lose the right of public discussion, the liberty of speech and the press, the law of evidence, trial by jury, and Habeas Corpus, throughout the indefinite peaceful future which I trust lies before them, any more than I am able to believe that a man could contract so strong an appetite for emetics during temporary illness, as to persist in feeding upon them through the remainder of his healthful life.

Letter to Erastus Corning and Others, [June 12,] 1863, reprinted in *Collected Works of Abraham Lincoln*, v. 6, p. 267. Rutgers University Press (1953, 1990).

By general law life *and* limb must be protected; yet often a limb must be amputated to save a life; but a life is never wisely given to save a limb.

Letter to Albert G. Hodges, April 4, 1864, reprinted in *Collected Works of Abraham Lincoln*, v. 7, p. 281. Rutgers University Press (1953, 1990).

CIVIL WAR

The Union, in any event, won't be dissolved. We don't want to dissolve it, and if you attempt it, *we won't let you.*

"Speech at Galena, Illinois," July 23, 1856, reprinted in *Collected Works of Abraham Lincoln*, v. 2, p. 355. Rutgers University Press (1953, 1990).

There will be no war, no violence.

"Seventh and Last Debate with Stephen A. Douglas at Alton, Illinois," October 15, 1858, reprinted in *Collected Works of Abraham Lincoln*, v. 3, p. 316. Rutgers University Press (1953, 1990).

There will be no blood shed unless it be forced upon the Government. The Government will not use force unless force is used against it.

"Speech in Independence Hall, Philadelphia, Pennsylvania," February 22, 1861, reprinted in *Collected Works of Abraham Lincoln*, v. 4, p. 241. Rutgers University Press (1953, 1990).

In *your* hands, my dissatisfied fellow countrymen, and not in *mine*, is the momentous issue of civil war.

"First Inaugural Address," March 4, 1861, reprinted in *Collected Works of Abraham Lincoln*, v. 4, p. 271. Rutgers University Press (1953, 1990).

This is essentially a People's contest. On the side of the Union, it is a struggle for maintaining in the world, that form and substance of government whose leading object is to elevate the condition of men—to lift artificial weights from all shoulders—to clear the paths of laudable pursuit for all, to afford all an unfettered start, and a fair chance, in the race of life.

"Message to Congress in Special Session," July 4, 1861, reprinted in *Collected Works of Abraham Lincoln*, v. 4, p. 438. Rutgers University Press (1953, 1990).

In the present civil war it is quite possible that God's purpose is something different from the purpose of either party. . . .

"Meditation on the Divine Will," [September 2, 1862?], reprinted in *Collected Works of Abraham Lincoln*, v. 5, p. 404. Rutgers University Press (1953, 1990).

It is easy to see that, under the sharp discipline of civil war, the nation is beginning a new life.

"Annual Message to Congress," December 8, 1863, reprinted in *Collected Works of Abraham Lincoln*, v. 7, p. 40. Rutgers University Press (1953, 1990).

Now, at the end of three years' struggle the nation's condition is not what either party, or any man devised, or expected. God alone can claim it.

Letter to Albert G. Hodges, April 4, 1864, reprinted in *Collected Works of Abraham Lincoln*, v. 7, p. 282. Rutgers University Press (1953, 1990).

In this the nation's day of trials, and also of its hopes.

"Remarks to One Hundred Thirtieth Ohio Regiment," June 11, 1864, reprinted in *Collected Works of Abraham Lincoln*, v. 7, p. 388. Rutgers University Press (1953, 1990).

An open field and a fair chance for your industry, enterprise and intelligence; that you may all have equal privileges in the race of life, with all its desirable human aspirations. It is for this the struggle should be maintained, that we may not lose our birthright. . . .

"Speech to One Hundred Sixty-Sixth Ohio Regiment," August 22, 1864, reprinted in *Collected Works of Abraham Lincoln*, v. 7, p. 512. Rutgers University Press (1953, 1990).

See also AMERICAN DREAM

This mighty convulsion, which no mortal could make, and no mortal could stay.

Letter to Eliza P. Gurney, September 4, 1864, reprinted in *Collected Works of Abraham Lincoln*, v. 7, p. 535. Rutgers University Press (1953, 1990).

Both parties deprecated war; but one of them would *make* war rather than let the nation survive; and the other would *accept* war rather than let it perish. And the war came.

"Second Inaugural Address," March 4, 1865, reprinted in *Collected Works of Abraham Lincoln*, v. 8, p. 332. Rutgers University Press (1953, 1990).

Both [sides in this war] read the same Bible, and pray to the same God; and each invokes His aid against the other.

"Second Inaugural Address," March 4, 1865, reprinted in *Collected Works of Abraham Lincoln*, v. 8, p. 333. Rutgers University Press (1953, 1990).

See also WAR; GOD

CLARITY

Feeling that his whole proposition was mere nonsense, he did not think of it distinctly enough to enable him to speak with any precision.

"Speech to the Springfield Scott Club," August 26, 1852, reprinted in *Collected Works of Abraham Lincoln*, v. 2, p. 140. Rutgers University Press (1953, 1990).

Referring to Senator Douglas.

As plain as the adding up of the weights of three small hogs.

Form letter to Fillmore men, September 8, 1856, reprinted in *Collected Works of Abraham Lincoln*, v. 2, p. 374. Rutgers University Press (1953, 1990).

Clear it of all the verbiage. . . .

"Speech at Columbus, Ohio," September 16, 1859, reprinted in *Collected Works of Abraham Lincoln*, v. 3, p. 417. Rutgers University Press (1953, 1990).

A criticism of Senator Douglas' arguments.

None can fail to see them, unless it may be those who are driven mad and blind by their sufferings.

Letter to John M. Fleming and Robert Morrow, August 9, 1863, reprinted in *Collected Works of Abraham Lincoln*, v. 6, p. 373. Rutgers University Press (1953, 1990).

On difficulties of getting Union armies into East Tennessee.

COLONELS

I personally wish Jacob R. Freese of New Jersey to be appointed a Colonel for a colored regiment—and this regardless of whether he can tell the exact shade of Julius Caesar's hair.

Letter to Edwin M. Stanton, November 11, 1863, reprinted in *Collected Works of Abraham Lincoln*, v. 7, p. 11. Rutgers University Press (1953, 1990).

COMMERCE

Commerce brings us together, and makes us better friends. We like one another the more for it.

"Seventh and Last Debate with Stephen A. Douglas at Alton, Illinois," October 15, 1858, reprinted in *Collected Works of Abraham Lincoln*, v. 3, p. 309. Rutgers University Press (1953, 1990).

COMMERCE: INTERNATIONAL

We must look not merely to *buying* cheap, not yet to buying cheap *and* selling dear; but also to having constant employment. . . .

"Fragments of a Tariff Discussion," [December 1, 1847?], reprinted in *Collected Works of Abraham Lincoln*, v. 1, p. 411. Rutgers University Press (1953, 1990).

COMMUNICATION

The inclination to exchange thoughts with one another is probably an original impulse of our nature.

"Second Lecture on Discoveries and Inventions," February 11, 1859, reprinted in *Collected Works of Abraham Lincoln*, v. 3, p. 359. Rutgers University Press (1953, 1990).

COMMUNITY

Of all things, avoid if possible, a dividing into cliques among the friends of the common object.

Letter to Frederick Steele, January 30, 1864, reprinted in *Collected Works of Abraham Lincoln*, v. 7, p. 161. Rutgers University Press (1953, 1990).

COMPETITION

If the gentleman from Fulton [an Illinois state legislator] thought that he was paying too high for his bread and meat, let him go home and invite his constituents to come over and set up a competition in this line of business.

"Speech in Illinois Legislature," January 25, 1841, reprinted in *Collected Works of Abraham Lincoln*, v. 1, p. 230. Rutgers University Press (1953, 1990).

Compliments

Every one likes a compliment. Thank you for yours. . . .

Letter to Thurlow Weed, March 15, 1865, reprinted in *Collected Works of Abraham Lincoln*, v. 8, p. 356. Rutgers University Press (1953, 1990).

Compromise

Persuade your neighbors to compromise whenever you can.

Fragment: "Notes for a Law Lecture," [July 1, 1850?], reprinted in *Collected Works of Abraham Lincoln*, v. 2, p. 81. Rutgers University Press (1953, 1990).

The spirit of concession and compromise—that spirit which has never failed us in past perils, and which may be safely trusted for all the future.

"Speech at Peoria, Illinois," October 16, 1854, reprinted in *Collected Works of Abraham Lincoln*, v. 2, p. 272. Rutgers University Press (1953, 1990).

Stand on middle ground and hold the ship level and steady.

"Speech at Peoria, Illinois," October 16, 1854, reprinted in *Collected Works of Abraham Lincoln*, vol. 2, p. 273. Rutgers University Press (1953, 1990).

Merely settlements of small phases of the question, not of the question itself.

"Speech at Bloomington, Illinois," September 4, 1858, reprinted in *Collected Works of Abraham Lincoln*, v. 3, p. 86. Rutgers University Press (1953, 1990).

Slavery dispute.

Conceit

Conceited whelp! we laugh at thee—
      Nor mind, that not a few
Of pompous, two-legged dogs there be,
      Conceited quite as you.

"The Bear Hunt," [c. September 1846?], reprinted in *Collected Works of Abraham Lincoln*, v. 1, p. 389. Rutgers University Press (1953, 1990).

CONFEDERATES

Our erring brethren. . . .

> "Speech to One Hundred Fortieth Indiana Regiment," March 17, 1865, reprinted in *Collected Works of Abraham Lincoln*, v. 8, p. 360. Rutgers University Press (1953, 1990).

CONFIDENCE

I suspect that [his] confidence is not more firmly fixed . . . than it was with the old woman, whose horse ran away with her in a buggy. She said she trusted in Providence till the britchen broke; and then she didn't know what on airth *to* do.

> "Speech to the Springfield Scott Club," August 26, 1852, reprinted in *Collected Works of Abraham Lincoln*, v. 2, p. 150. Rutgers University Press (1953, 1990).
>
> Referring to Senator Douglas.

CONFIDENTIALITY

This letter is, of course, confidential; tho I should have no objection to its being seen by a few friends, in your discretion, being *sure* first that they are friends.

> Letter to Benjamin F. James, December 6, 1845, reprinted in *Collected Works of Abraham Lincoln, Supplement 1832-1865*, v. 10, p. 9. Rutgers University Press (1953, 1990).
>
> Plans for congressional nomination.

I think you would better not make this letter public; but you may rely confidently on my standing by whatever I have said in it.

> Letter to John A. McClernand, January 8, 1863, reprinted in *Collected Works of Abraham Lincoln*, v. 6, p. 49. Rutgers University Press (1953, 1990).

The publication of a letter without the leave of the writer or the receiver I think cannot be justified, but . . . I do not think it of sufficient consequence to justify an arrest. . . .

> Letter to Henry T. Blow, July 13, 1863, reprinted in *Collected Works of Abraham Lincoln*, v. 6, p. 325. Rutgers University Press (1953, 1990).

CONFISCATION

You speak of it [General John Fremont's order freeing slaves in Missouri] as being the only means of *saving* the government. On the contrary it is itself the surrender of the government. Can it be pretended that it is any longer the government of the U.S.—any government of Constitution and laws,—wherein a General, or a President, may make permanent rules of property by proclamation?

> Letter to Orville H. Browning, September 22, 1861, reprinted in *Collected Works of Abraham Lincoln*, v. 4, p. 532. Rutgers University Press (1953, 1990).

CONFORMITY

Let me ask the man . . . what compensation he will accept to go to church some Sunday and sit during the sermon with his wife's bonnet upon his head? Not a trifle, I'll venture.

> "Temperance Address," February 22, 1842, reprinted in *Collected Works of Abraham Lincoln*, v. 1, p. 277. Rutgers University Press (1953, 1990).

CONSCRIPTION

Necessity knows no law.

> Letter to Alexander Ramsey, August 27, 1862, reprinted in *Collected Works of Abraham Lincoln*, v. 5, p. 396. Rutgers University Press (1953, 1990).

CONSEQUENCES AND REGRETS

Now, sir, there is in this so much assumption of facts, and so much of menace as to consequences, that I cannot submit to answer that note any farther than I have, and to add, that the consequence to which I suppose you allude, would be matter of as great regret to me as it possibly could to you.

> Letter to James Shields, September 17, 1842, reprinted in *Collected Works of Abraham Lincoln*, v. 1, p. 299. Rutgers University Press (1953, 1990).
>
> From correspondence leading up to a near duel.

CONSERVATISM

In anciently inhabited countries, the dust of ages—a real downright old-fogyism—seems to settle upon, and smother the intellects and energies of man.

"Second Lecture on Discoveries and Inventions," February 11, 1859, reprinted in *Collected Works of Abraham Lincoln*, v. 3, p. 363. Rutgers University Press (1953, 1990).

What is conservatism? Is it not adherence to the old and tried, against the new and untried?

"Speech at New Haven, Connecticut," March 5, 1860, reprinted in *Collected Works of Abraham Lincoln*, v. 4, p. 27. Rutgers University Press (1953, 1990).

I hope to "stand firm" enough to not go backward, and yet not go forward fast enough to wreck the country's cause.

Letter to Zachariah Chandler, November 20, 1863, reprinted in *Collected Works of Abraham Lincoln*, v. 7, p. 24. Rutgers University Press (1953, 1990).

CONSTITUTION OF THE UNITED STATES

As a general rule, I think, we would [do] much better [to] let it alone. No slight occasion should tempt us to touch it [with an amendment].

"Speech in the United States House of Representatives on Internal Improvements," June 20, 1848, reprinted in *Collected Works of Abraham Lincoln*, v. 1, p. 488. Rutgers University Press (1953, 1990).

Nothing in the Constitution or laws of any State can destroy a right distinctly and expressly affirmed in the Constitution of the United States.

"Fifth Debate with Stephen A. Douglas, at Galesburg, Illinois," October 7, 1858, reprinted in *Collected Works of Abraham Lincoln*, v. 3, p. 231. Rutgers University Press (1953, 1990).

[Senator Stephen A. Douglas] is bound to support it [the Constitution] as he understands it. I understand it another way, and therefore I am bound to support it in the way in which I understand it.

"Sixth Debate with Stephen A. Douglas, at Quincy, Illinois," October 13, 1858, reprinted in *Collected Works of Abraham Lincoln*, v. 3, p. 278. Rutgers University Press (1953, 1990).

The Constitution is as silent about that, as it is silent personally about myself.

"Speech at Cincinnati, Ohio," September 17, 1859, reprinted in *Collected Works of Abraham Lincoln*, v. 3, p. 448. Rutgers University Press (1953, 1990).

On secession. See also SECESSION

But no organic law can ever be framed with a provision specifically applicable to every question which may occur in practical administration. No foresight can anticipate, nor any document of reasonable length contain express provisions for all possible questions.

"First Inaugural Address," March 4, 1861, reprinted in *Collected Works of Abraham Lincoln*, v. 4, p. 267. Rutgers University Press (1953, 1990).

This amendment [abolishing slavery] is a King's cure for all the evils. It winds the whole thing up.

"Response to a Serenade," February 1, 1865, reprinted in *Collected Works of Abraham Lincoln*, v. 8, p. 254. Rutgers University Press (1953, 1990).

COOPERATION

We can succeed only by concert.

"Annual Message to Congress," December 1, 1860, reprinted in *Collected Works of Abraham Lincoln*, v. 5, p. 537. Rutgers University Press (1953, 1990).

COURT PACKING

The Supreme Court of Illinois, consisting of four judges, because of one decision made, and one expected to be made, were overwhelmed by the adding of five new judges to their number. . . . How far a court, so constituted, is prostituted beneath the contempt of all men. . . .

Fragment: "Notes for Speeches," [c. August 21, 1858], reprinted in *Collected Works of Abraham Lincoln*, v. 2, p. 552. Rutgers University Press (1953, 1990).

See also LAW

Courts

I fear ... "A Puppy Court". ... "A Migratory [state] Supreme Court" and *Salaries* so low as to exclude all respectable talent. From these, may God preserve us.

Letter to Orville H. Browning, June 24, 1847, reprinted in *Collected Works of Abraham Lincoln*, v. 1, p. 394. Rutgers University Press (1953, 1990).

Some other things I have fears for. I am not easy about the *Courts*. I am satisfied with them as they are; but shall not care *much* if the judges are made elective by the People, and their terms of office limited.

 Letter to Orville H. Browning, June 24, 1847, reprinted in *Collected Works of Abraham Lincoln*, v. 1, p. 394. Rutgers University Press (1953, 1990).

Deals

If such persons have what will be an advantage to them, the question is whether it cannot be made of advantage to you.

 "Address on Colonization to a Deputation of Negroes," August 14, 1862, reprinted in *Collected Works of Abraham Lincoln*, v. 5, p. 374. Rutgers University Press (1953, 1990).

Death

I hear the loved survivors tell
  How naught from death could save,
Till every sound appears a knell,
  And every spot a grave.

I range the fields with pensive tread,
  And pace the hollow rooms,
And feel (companion of the dead)
  I'm living in the tombs.

 "My Childhood's Home," September 18, 1846, reprinted in *Collected Works of Abraham Lincoln*, v. 1, p. 379. Rutgers University Press (1953, 1990).

As is appointed to all men once to do, he died.

"Speech to the Springfield Scott Club," August 26, 1852, reprinted in *Collected Works of Abraham Lincoln*, v. 2, p. 150. Rutgers University Press (1953, 1990).

It is with deep grief that I learn of the death of your kind and brave Father; and, especially, that it is affecting your young heart beyond what is common in such cases. . . . The memory of your dear Father, instead of an agony, will yet be a sad sweet feeling in your heart, of a purer, and holier sort than you have known before.

Letter to Fanny McCullough, December 23, 1862, reprinted in *Collected Works of Abraham Lincoln*, v. 6, p. 16. Rutgers University Press (1953, 1990).

See also WAR DEAD

*D*EBT: *GOVERNMENT'S*

There was another objection to this plan . . . [the] impropriety of borrowing money to pay interest on borrowed money—that we are hereby paying compound interest. To this he would reply, that if it were a fact that our population and wealth were increasing in a ratio greater than the increased interest hereby incurred, then this was not a good objection.

"Remarks in Illinois Legislature," December 4, 1840, reprinted in *Collected Works of Abraham Lincoln*, v. 1, p. 216. Rutgers University Press (1953, 1990).

A new national debt, has been created, and is still growing on us with a rapidity fearful to contemplate—a rapidity only reasonably to be expected in time of war.

"Campaign Circular from Whig Committee," March 4, 1843, reprinted in *Collected Works of Abraham Lincoln*, v. 1, p. 311. Rutgers University Press (1953, 1990).

As an individual who undertakes to live by borrowing, soon finds his original means devoured by interest, and next no one left to borrow from—so must it be with a government.

"Campaign Circular from Whig Committee," March 4, 1843, reprinted in *Collected Works of Abraham Lincoln*, v. 1, p. 311. Rutgers University Press (1953, 1990).

The system of loans is but temporary in its nature, and must soon explode. It is a system, not only ruinous while it lasts, but one that must soon fail and leave us destitute.

"Campaign Circular from Whig Committee," March 4, 1843, reprinted in *Collected Works of Abraham Lincoln*, v. 1, p. 311. Rutgers University Press (1953, 1990).

I would not borrow money. I am against an overwhelming, crushing system.

"Speech in United States House of Representatives on Internal Improvements," June 20, 1848, reprinted in *Collected Works of Abraham Lincoln*, v. 1, p. 489. Rutgers University Press (1953, 1990).

Time alone relieves a debtor nation, so long as its population increases faster than unpaid interest accumulates on its debt.

"Annual Message to Congress," December 1, 1862, reprinted in *Collected Works of Abraham Lincoln*, v. 5, p. 534. Rutgers University Press (1953, 1990).

Men readily perceive that they cannot be much oppressed by a debt which they owe to themselves.

"Annual Message to Congress," December 6, 1864, reprinted in *Collected Works of Abraham Lincoln*, v. 8, p. 143. Rutgers University Press (1953, 1990).

DECLARATION OF INDEPENDENCE

The fourth of July has not quite dwindled away; it is still a great day— *for burning fire-crackers!!!*

Letter to George Robertson, August 15, 1855, reprinted in *Collected Works of Abraham Lincoln*, v. 2, p. 318. Rutgers University Press (1953, 1990).

In those days [of yore], our Declaration of Independence was held sacred by all, and thought to include all; but now, to aid in making the bondage of the negro universal and eternal, it is assailed, and sneered at, and construed, and hawked at, and torn, till, if its framers could rise from their graves, they could not at all recognize it.

"Speech at Springfield, Illinois," June 26, 1857, reprinted in *Collected Works of Abraham Lincoln*, v. 2, p. 404. Rutgers University Press (1953, 1990).

[The Declaration of Independence] meant to set up a standard maxim for free society, which should be familiar to all, and revered by all; constantly looked to, constantly labored for, and even though never perfectly attained, constantly approximated, and thereby constantly spreading and deepening its influence, and augmenting the happiness and value of life to all people of all colors everywhere.

"Speech at Springfield, Illinois," June 26, 1857, reprinted in *Collected Works of Abraham Lincoln*, v. 2, p. 406. Rutgers University Press (1953, 1990).

A stumbling block to those who in after times might seek to turn a free people back into the hateful paths of despotism.

"Speech at Springfield, Illinois," June 26, 1857, reprinted in *Collected Works of Abraham Lincoln*, v. 2, p. 406. Rutgers University Press (1953, 1990).

The Declaration contemplated the progressive improvement in the condition of all men everywhere. . . .

"Speech at Springfield, Illinois," June 26, 1857, reprinted in *Collected Works of Abraham Lincoln*, v. 2, p. 407. Rutgers University Press (1953, 1990).

I believe the declaration that "all men are created equal" is the great fundamental principle upon which our free institutions rest. . . .

Letter to James N. Brown, October 18, 1858, reprinted in *Collected Works of Abraham Lincoln*, v. 3, p. 327. Rutgers University Press (1953, 1990).

I have never had a feeling politically that did not spring from the sentiments embodied in the Declaration of Independence.

"Speech in Independence Hall, Philadelphia, Pennsylvania," February 22, 1861, reprinted in *Collected Works of Abraham Lincoln*, v. 4, p. 240. Rutgers University Press (1953, 1990).

Four score and seven years ago our fathers brought forth on this continent, a new nation, conceived in Liberty, and dedicated to the proposition that all men are created equal.

Now we are engaged in a great civil war, testing whether that nation, or any nation so conceived and so dedicated, can long endure.

"Gettysburg Address," November 19, 1863, reprinted in *Collected Works of Abraham Lincoln*, v. 7, p. 23. Rutgers University Press (1953, 1990).

*D*ELUSION

Delusion gross as insanity itself.

"Notes for Speeches at Columbus and Cincinnati, Ohio," [September 16–17, 1859], reprinted in *Collected Works of Abraham Lincoln*, v. 3, p. 432. Rutgers University Press (1953, 1990).

*D*EMANDS

He says he can not live if he goes home without it [appointment to office], and I don't think I can live if he stays here. I am serious about this.

Letter to Edwin M. Stanton, December 21, 1863, reprinted in *Collected Works of Abraham Lincoln*, v. 10, p. 213. Rutgers University Press (1953, 1990).

On an office seeker.

*D*EMOCRACY

No man is good enough to govern another man, *without that other's consent.* I say this is the leading principle—the sheet anchor of American republicanism.

"Speech at Peoria, Illinois," October 16, 1854, reprinted in *Collected Works of Abraham Lincoln*, v. 2, p. 266. Rutgers University Press (1953, 1990).

As I would not be a *slave*, so I would not be a *master*. This expresses my idea of democracy. Whatever differs from this, to the extent of the difference, is no democracy.

Definition of Democracy, August 1, 1858?, reprinted in *Collected Works of Abraham Lincoln*, v. 2, p. 532. Rutgers University Press (1953, 1990).

Why should there not be a patient confidence in the ultimate justice of the people? Is there any better or equal hope, in the world?

"First Inaugural Address"—First Edition and Revisions, March 4, 1861, reprinted in *Collected Works of Abraham Lincoln*, v. 4, p. 260. Rutgers University Press (1953, 1990).

Government of the people, by the people, for the people. . . .

"Gettysburg Address," November 19, 1863, reprinted in *Collected Works of Abraham Lincoln*, v. 7, p.23. Rutgers University Press (1953, 1990).

*D*EMOCRATIC PARTY

If they think they are able to slander a woman into loving them, or a man into voting with them, they will learn better presently.

"Speech at Hartford, Connecticut," March 5, 1860, reprinted in *Collected Works of Abraham Lincoln*, v. 4, p. 7. Rutgers University Press (1953, 1990).

*D*ENIALS

He denied, and denied, and persisted in denying.

"The Trailor Murder Case," April 15, 1846, reprinted in *Collected Works of Abraham Lincoln*, v. 1, p. 373. Rutgers University Press (1953, 1990).

*D*ENUNCIATION

I regret to find you denouncing so many persons as liars, scoundrels, fools, thieves, and persecutors of yourself.

Letter to James G. Blunt, August 18, 1863, reprinted in *Collected Works of Abraham Lincoln*, v. 6, p. 396. Rutgers University Press (1953, 1990).

*D*EPRESSION

Remember in the depth and even the agony of despondency, that very shortly you are to feel well again.

Letter to Joshua F. Speed, February 13, 1842, reprinted in *Collected Works of Abraham Lincoln*, v. 1, p. 269. Rutgers University Press (1953, 1990).

You can not now realize that you will ever feel better. Is not this so? And yet it is a mistake.

> Letter to Fanny McCullough, December 23, 1862, reprinted in *Collected Works of Abraham Lincoln*, v. 6, p. 17. Rutgers University Press (1953, 1990).

See also MELANCHOLY

*D*ESERTION

He who dissuades one man from volunteering, or induces one soldier to desert, weakens the Union cause as much as he who kills a union soldier in battle.

> Letter to Erastus Corning and Others, [June 12], 1863, reprinted in *Collected Works of Abraham Lincoln*, v. 6, p. 264. Rutgers University Press (1953, 1990).

Must I shoot a simple-minded soldier boy who deserts, while I must not touch a hair of a wily agitator who induces him to desert?

> Letter to Erastus Corning and Others, [June 12], 1863, reprinted in *Collected Works of Abraham Lincoln*, v. 6, p. 266. Rutgers University Press (1953, 1990).

Let him fight instead of being shot.

> Letter to Joseph Holt, July 18, 1863, reprinted in *Collected Works of Abraham Lincoln*, v. 6, p. 335. Rutgers University Press (1953, 1990).

See also PARDONS

*D*ESPOTISM

When the white man governs himself that is self-government; but when he governs himself, and also governs *another* man, that is *more* than self-government—that is despotism.

> "Speech at Peoria, Illinois," October 16, 1854, reprinted in *Collected Works of Abraham Lincoln*, v. 2, p. 266. Rutgers University Press (1953, 1990).

Our progress in degeneracy appears to me to be pretty rapid. As a nation, we began by declaring that *"all men are created equal."* We now practically read it "all men are created equal, *except Negroes."* When the Know-Nothings get control, it will read "all men are created equal, except negroes, *and foreigners, and catholics."* When it comes to this I should prefer emigrating to some country where they make no pretense of loving liberty—to Russia, for instance, where despotism can be taken pure, and without the base alloy of hypocrisy.

Letter to Joshua F. Speed, August 24, 1855, reprinted in *Collected Works of Abraham Lincoln*, v. 2, p. 323. Rutgers University Press (1953, 1990).

See also DECLARATION OF INDEPENDENCE

*D*ETERMINATION

Determine that the thing can and shall be done, and then we shall find the way.

"Speech in United States House of Representatives on Internal Improvements," June 20, 1848, reprinted in *Collected Works of Abraham Lincoln*, v. 1, p. 489. Rutgers University Press (1953, 1990).

The boy who was talking to another as to whether General [Andrew] Jackson could ever get to Heaven: Said the boy "He'd get there if he had a mind to."

"Speech at a Republican Banquet," Chicago, Illinois, December 10, 1856, reprinted in *Collected Works of Abraham Lincoln*, v. 2, p. 384. Rutgers University Press (1953, 1990).

Let us have faith that right makes might, and in that faith, let us, to the end, dare to do our duty as we understand it.

"Address at Cooper Institute, New York City," February 27, 1860, reprinted in *Collected Works of Abraham Lincoln*, v. 3, p. 550. Rutgers University Press (1953, 1990).

If you falter, and give up, you will lose the power of keeping any resolution, and will regret it all your life.

Letter to Quintin Campbell, June 28, 1862, reprinted in *Collected Works of Abraham Lincoln*, v. 5, p. 288. Rutgers University Press (1953, 1990).

I expect to maintain this contest until successful, or till I die, or am conquered, or my term expires, or Congress or the country forsakes me. . . .

Letter to William H. Seward, June 29, 1862, reprinted in *Collected Works of Abraham Lincoln*, v. 5, p. 292. Rutgers University Press (1953, 1990).

I must save this government if possible. What I *cannot* do, of course I *will* not do; but it may as well be understood, once for all, that I shall not surrender this game leaving any available card unplayed.

Letter to Reverdy Johnson, July 26, 1862, reprinted in *Collected Works of Abraham Lincoln*, v. 5, p. 343. Rutgers University Press (1953, 1990).

*D*ICTATORSHIP

I have heard, in such way as to believe it, of your recently saying that both the Army and the Government needed a Dictator. Of course it was not *for* this, but in spite of it, that I have given you the command. Only those generals who gain successes, can set up dictators. What I now ask of you is military success, and I will risk the dictatorship.

Letter to General Joseph Hooker, January 26, 1863, reprinted in *Collected Works of Abraham Lincoln*, v. 6, p. 78. Rutgers University Press (1953, 1990).

*D*IFFERENCES

Let bygones be bygones. Let past differences, as nothing be. . . .

"Speech at a Republican Banquet, Chicago, Illinois," December 10, 1856, reprinted in *Collected Works of Abraham Lincoln*, v. 2, p. 385. Rutgers University Press (1953, 1990).

*D*ILIGENCE

The leading rule for the lawyer, as for the man of every other calling, is diligence. Leave nothing for to-morrow which can be done to-day.

Fragment: "Notes For a Law Lecture," [July 1, 1850?], reprinted in *Collected Works of Abraham Lincoln*, v. 2, p. 81. Rutgers University Press (1953, 1990).

*D*ISAGREEMENT

The subject is difficult, and good men do not agree.

> Reply to "Emancipation Memorial Presented by Chicago Christians of All Denominations,"
> September 13, 1862, reprinted in *Collected Works of Abraham Lincoln*, v. 5, p. 420. Rutgers University
> Press (1953, 1990)
>
> On timing of emancipation.

Instead of settling one dispute by deciding the question, I should merely furnish a nest full of eggs for hatching new disputes.

> Letter to Edward Bates, November 29, 1862, reprinted in *Collected Works of Abraham Lincoln*, v. 5,
> p. 516. Rutgers University Press (1953, 1990).
>
> On infighting among Missouri Unionists.

Surely you do not mean to understand that I am withholding my confidence from you when I happen to express an opinion (certainly never discourteously) differing from one of your own.

> Letter to General Joseph Hooker, June 16, 1863, reprinted in *Collected Works of Abraham Lincoln*, v. 6, p.
> 281. Rutgers University Press (1953, 1990).

*D*ISCOVERIES

All creation is a mine, and every man, a miner.

> "First Lecture on Discoveries and Inventions," April 6, 1858, reprinted in *Collected Works of Abraham
> Lincoln*, v. 2, p. 437. Rutgers University Press (1953, 1990).

I know nothing so pleasant to the mind, as the discovery of anything which is at once *new* and *valuable*—nothing which so lightens and sweetens toil, as the hopeful pursuit of such discovery.

> "Address before the Wisconsin State Agricultural Society," Milwaukee, Wisconsin, September 30, 1859,
> reprinted in *Collected Works of Abraham Lincoln*, v. 3, p. 480. Rutgers University Press (1953, 1990)

What one observes, and would himself infer nothing from, he tells to another, and that other at once sees a valuable hint in it. A result is thus reached which neither *alone* would have arrived at.

> "Second Lecture on Discoveries and Inventions," February 11, 1859, reprinted in *Collected Works of
> Abraham Lincoln*, v. 3, p. 360. Rutgers University Press (1953, 1990).

*D*ISHONESTY

However much care selections may be made, there will be some unfaithful and dishonest. . . . The experience of the whole world, in all bygone times, proves this true. The Savior of the world chose twelve disciples, and even one of that small number, selected by superhuman wisdom, turned out a traitor and a devil.

> "Speech on the Sub-Treasury," December 26, 1839, reprinted in *Collected Works of Abraham Lincoln*, v. 1, p. 167. Rutgers University Press (1953, 1990).

Who that knows anything of human nature, doubts that, in many instances, interest will prevail over duty. . . .

> "Speech on the Sub-Treasury," December 26, 1839, reprinted in *Collected Works of Abraham Lincoln*, v. 1, p. 167. Rutgers University Press (1953, 1990).
>
> See also LIES

*D*ISHONOR

I would as soon put my head in the fire as to attempt it.

> Letter to Martin S. Morris, April 14, 1843, reprinted in *Collected Works of Abraham Lincoln*, v. 1, p. 321. Rutgers University Press (1953, 1990).
>
> Referring to self-promotion.

*D*IVORCE *(FROM REBEL)*

I would not offer her, or any wife, a temptation to a permanent separation from her husband; but if she shall avow that her mind is already, independently and fully made up to such separation, I shall be glad for the property sought by her letter, to be delivered to her. . . .

> Letter to Whom It May Concern, April 11, 1864, reprinted in *Collected Works of Abraham Lincoln*, v. 7, p. 296. Rutgers University Press (1953, 1990).

*D*IXIE

I have always thought "Dixie" one of the best tunes I have ever heard. Our adversaries over the way attempted to appropriate it, but I insisted yesterday that we fairly captured it. I presented the question to the

Attorney General, and he gave it as his legal opinion that it is our lawful prize. I now request the band to favor me with its performance.

"Response to Serenade," April 10, 1865, reprinted in *Collected Works of Abraham Lincoln*, v. 8, p. 393. Rutgers University Press (1953, 1990).

*D*OUGLAS, STEPHEN A.

With *me*, the race of ambition has been a failure—a flat failure; with *him* it has been one of splendid success. His name fills the nation and is not unknown, even in foreign lands. I affect no contempt for the high eminence he has reached. So reached, that the oppressed of my species might have shared with me in the elevation, I would rather stand on that eminence than wear the richest crown that ever pressed a monarch's brow.

"Fragment on Stephen A. Douglas," c. December 1856, reprinted in *Collected Works of Abraham Lincoln*, v. 2, p. 383. Rutgers University Press (1953, 1990).

A *living* dog is better than a *dead lion*. Judge Douglas, if not a *dead lion* for *this work* [of opposing the expansion of slavery], is at least a *caged* and a *toothless* one.

"A House Divided," Speech at Springfield, Illinois, June 16, 1858,

His explanations explanatory of explanations explained are interminable.

"Speech at Columbus, Ohio," September 16, 1859, reprinted in *Collected Works of Abraham Lincoln*, v. 3, p. 405. Rutgers University Press (1953, 1990).

*E*CONOMIC DEPRESSION

In the midst of our almost insupportable difficulties, in the days of our severest necessity....

"Campaign Circular from Whig Committee," March 4, 1843, reprinted in *Collected Works of Abraham Lincoln*, v. 1, p. 312. Rutgers University Press (1953, 1990).

*E*CONOMIC DIVERSITY

They are the very cements of this Union. They don't make the house a house divided against itself. They are the props that hold up the house and sustain the Union.

"Third Debate with Stephen A. Douglas at Jonesboro, Illinois," September 15, 1858, reprinted in *Collected Works of Abraham Lincoln*, v. 3, p. 120. Rutgers University Press (1953, 1990).

ECONOMICS AND LAW

The variety in the soil and climate and face of the country, and consequent variety in the industrial pursuits and productions of a country, require systems of law conforming to this variety in the natural features of the country.

"Seventh and Last Debate with Stephen A. Douglas at Alton, Illinois," October 15, 1858, reprinted in *Collected Works of Abraham Lincoln*, v. 3, p. 309. Rutgers University Press (1953, 1990).

ECONOMISTS

There is a difference of opinion among political economists....

"Speech at Indianapolis, Indiana," September 19, 1859, reprinted in *Collected Works of Abraham Lincoln*, v. 3, p. 468. Rutgers University Press (1953, 1990).

ECONOMY

Economy is to be the order of the day.

Remarks in Illinois Legislature, January 17, 1839, reprinted in *Collected Works of Abraham Lincoln*, v. 1, p. 134. Rutgers University Press (1953, 1990).

EDITING

So far as it is intended merely to improve in grammar, and elegance of composition, I am quite agreed; but I do not wish the sense changed, or modified, to a hair's breadth. And you, not having studied the particular points so closely as I have, can not be quite sure that you do not change the sense when you do not intend it.

Letter to Charles C. Nott, May 31, 1860, reprinted in *Collected Works of Abraham Lincoln*, v. 4, p. 58. Rutgers University Press (1953, 1990).

*E*DUCATION

I view it as the most important subject which we as a people can be engaged in.

"Communication to the People of Sangamo County," March 9, 1832, reprinted in *Collected Works of Abraham Lincoln*, v. 1, p. 8. Rutgers University Press (1953, 1990).

In this country, one can scarcely be so poor, but that, if he *will*, he *can* acquire sufficient education to get through the world respectably.

"Eulogy on Henry Clay," July 6, 1852, reprinted in *Collected Works of Abraham Lincoln*, v. 2, p. 124. Rutgers University Press (1953, 1990).

Every head should be cultivated. . . .

"Address before the Wisconsin State Agricultural Society, Milwaukee, Wisconsin," September 30, 1859, reprinted in *Collected Works of Abraham Lincoln*, v. 3, p. 480. Rutgers University Press (1953, 1990).

*E*DUCATION: *LAWYER'S*

If you wish to be a lawyer, attach no consequence to the *place* you are in, or the *person* [teacher-mentor] you are with; but get books, sit down anywhere, and go to reading for yourself. That will make a lawyer of you quicker than any other way.

Letter to William H. Grigsby, August 3, 1858, reprinted in *Collected Works of Abraham Lincoln*, v. 2, p. 535. Rutgers University Press (1953, 1990).

See also LAWYERS

*E*DUCATION AND LABOR

A Yankee who could invent a strong *handed* man without a head would receive the everlasting gratitude of the "mud-sill" advocates [pro-slavery opponents of free labor].

"Address before the Wisconsin State Agricultural Society, Milwaukee, Wisconsin," September 30, 1859, reprinted in *Collected Works of Abraham Lincoln*, v. 3, p. 479. Rutgers University Press (1953, 1990).

By the "mud-sill" theory it is assumed that labor and education are incompatible; and any practical combination of them impossible. According to that theory, a blind horse upon a treadmill, is a perfect illustration of what a laborer should be—all the better for being blind, that he could not tread out of place, or kick understandingly.

"Address before the Wisconsin State Agricultural Society, Milwaukee, Wisconsin," September 30, 1859, reprinted in *Collected Works of Abraham Lincoln*, v. 3, p. 479. Rutgers University Press (1953, 1990).

Free Labor insists on universal education.

"Address before the Wisconsin State Agricultural Society, Milwaukee, Wisconsin," September 30, 1859, reprinted in *Collected Works of Abraham Lincoln*, v. 3, p. 480. Rutgers University Press (1953, 1990)

Heads are regarded as explosive materials [by the opponents of free labor], only to be safely kept in damp places, as far as possible from that peculiar sort of fire which ignites them.

"Address before the Wisconsin State Agricultural Society, Milwaukee, Wisconsin," September 30, 1859, reprinted in *Collected Works of Abraham Lincoln*, v. 3, p. 479. Rutgers University Press (1953, 1990).

See also LABOR.

*E*LECTIONS

It is a long time till the election; and what may turn up, no one can tell.

Letter to John M. Palmer, August 1, 1856, reprinted in *Collected Works of Abraham Lincoln*, v. 2, p. 357. Rutgers University Press (1953, 1990).

Our only chance is with [Zachary] Taylor. I go for him, not because I think he would make a better president than Clay, but because I think he would make a better one than Polk, or Cass, or Buchanan, or any such creatures, one of whom is sure to be elected, if he is not.

Letter to Jesse Lynch, April 10, 1848, reprinted in *Collected Works of Abraham Lincoln*, v. 1, p. 463. Rutgers University Press (1953, 1990).

To give the victory to the right, not *bloody bullets,* but *peaceful ballots* only, are necessary.

"Fragment of a Speech," [c. May 18, 1858], reprinted in *Collected Works of Abraham Lincoln*, v. 2, p. 454. Rutgers University Press (1953, 1990).

I do not deny the possibility that the people may err in an election; but if they do, the true cure is in the next election. . . .

Fragment of "Speech Intended for Kentuckians," [c. February 12, 1861], reprinted in *Collected Works of Abraham Lincoln*, v. 4, p. 201. Rutgers University Press (1953, 1990).

For the result of an election, held in military camps, where the bayonets are all on one side of the question voted upon, can scarcely be considered as demonstrating popular sentiment.

"Message to Congress in Special Session," July 4, 1861, reprinted in *Collected Works of Abraham Lincoln*, v. 4, p. 437. Rutgers University Press (1953, 1990).

Peace does not appear so distant as it did. I hope it will come soon, and come to stay; and so come as to be worth the keeping in all future time. It will then have been proved that, among free men, there can be no successful appeal from the ballot to the bullet; and that they who take such appeal are sure to lose their case, and pay the cost.

Letter to James C. Conkling, August 26, 1863, reprinted in *Collected Works of Abraham Lincoln*, v. 6, p. 410. Rutgers University Press (1953, 1990).

There can be no successful appeal from a fair election, but to the next election.

Fragment, [c. August 26, 1863?] , reprinted in *Collected Works of Abraham Lincoln*, v. 6, p. 410. Rutgers University Press (1953, 1990).

This morning, as for some days past, it seems exceedingly probable that this Administration will not be reelected. Then it will be my duty to so cooperate with the President elect, as to save the Union between the election and the inauguration; as he will have secured his election on such ground that he can not possibly save it afterwards.

"Memorandum Concerning His Probable Failure of Reelection," August 23, 1864, reprinted in *Collected Works of Abraham Lincoln*, v. 7, p. 514. Rutgers University Press (1953, 1990).

The election was a necessity. We can not have free government without elections; and if the rebellion could force us to forego, or postpone a national election, it might fairly claim to have already conquered and ruined us. . . . The election, along with its incidental, and undesirable strife, has done good too. It has demonstrated that a people's government can sustain a national election, in the midst of a great civil war.

"Response to a Serenade," November 10, 1864, reprinted in *Collected Works of Abraham Lincoln*, v. 8, p. 101. Rutgers University Press (1953, 1990).

The strife of the election is but human nature practically applied to the facts of the case.

"Response to a Serenade," November 10, 1864, reprinted in *Collected Works of Abraham Lincoln*, v. 8, p. 101. Rutgers University Press (1953, 1990).

Now that the election is over, may not all, having a common interest, reunite in a common effort, to save our common country?

> "Response to a Serenade," November 10, 1864, reprinted in *Collected Works of Abraham Lincoln*, v. 8, p. 101. Rutgers University Press (1953, 1990).

*E*LOQUENCE

He was surpassingly eloquent; but many eloquent men fail utterly; and they are not, as a class, generally successful.

> "Eulogy on Henry Clay," July 6, 1852, reprinted in *Collected Works of Abraham Lincoln*, v. 2, p. 125. Rutgers University Press (1953, 1990).

*E*MANCIPATION

Perhaps the best way for it [slavery] to come to an end peaceably is for it to exist for a length of time.

> "Speech at Chicago, Illinois," March 1, 1859, reprinted in *Collected Works of Abraham Lincoln*, v. 3, p. 370. Rutgers University Press (1953, 1990).

For instance, out in the street, or in the field, or on the prairie I find a rattlesnake. I take a stake and kill him. Everybody would applaud the act and say I did right. But suppose the snake was in a bed where children were sleeping. Would I do right to strike him there? I might hurt the children; or I might not kill, but only arouse and exasperate the snake, and he might bite the children. Thus, by meddling with him here, I would do more hurt than good. Slavery is like this. We dare not strike at it where it is.

> "Speech at Hartford, Connecticut," March 5, 1860, reprinted in *Collected Works of Abraham Lincoln*, v. 4, p. 5. Rutgers University Press (1953, 1990).

I do not want to issue a document that the whole world will see must necessarily be inoperative, like the Pope's bull against the comet!

> "Reply to Chicago Christians," September 13, 1862, reprinted in *Collected Works of Abraham Lincoln*, v. 5, p. 420. Rutgers University Press (1953, 1990).
>
> Reply to delegation claiming God wanted emancipation. See also GOD.

Shall be then, thenceforward, and forever free. . . .

"Preliminary Emancipation Proclamation," September 22, 1862, reprinted in *Collected Works of Abraham Lincoln*, v. 5, p. 434. Rutgers University Press (1953, 1990).

Fellow citizens, *we* cannot escape history. We of this Congress and this administration will be remembered in spite of ourselves. No personal significance, or insignificance, can spare one or another of us. The fiery trial through which we pass will light us down, in honor or dishonor, to the latest generation. We *say* we are for the Union. The world will not forget that we say this. We know how to save the Union. The world knows we do know how to save it. We—even *we here*—hold the power, and bear the responsibility. In *giving* freedom to the *slave*, we *assure* freedom to the *free*—honorable alike in what we give, and what we preserve. We shall nobly save, or meanly lose, the last best hope of earth. Other means may succeed; this could not fail. The way is plain, peaceful, generous, just—a way which, if followed, the world will forever applaud, and God must forever bless.

"Annual Message to Congress," December 1, 1862, reprinted in *Collected Works of Abraham Lincoln*, v. 5, p. 537. Rutgers University Press (1953, 1990).

While commendation in newspapers and by distinguished individuals is all that a vain man could wish, the stocks have declined, and troops come forward more slowly than ever.

Letter to Hannibal Hamlin, September 28, 1862, reprinted in *Collected Works of Abraham Lincoln*, v. 5, p. 444. Rutgers University Press (1953, 1990).

Hailed by some as the advance of liberty, and bewailed by others as the destruction of all liberty.

"Address at Sanitary Fair," Baltimore, Maryland, April 18, 1864, reprinted in *Collected Works of Abraham Lincoln*, v. 7, p. 302. Rutgers University Press (1953, 1990).

*E*MBARRASSMENT

I have found that when one is embarrassed, usually the shortest way to get through with it is to quit talking or thinking about it, and go at something else.

"Speech at Cincinnati, Ohio," September 17, 1859, reprinted in *Collected Works of Abraham Lincoln*, v. 3, p. 438. Rutgers University Press (1953, 1990).

*E*MPLOYMENT

We must look not merely to *buying* cheap, nor yet to buying cheap *and* selling dear, but also to having constant employment....

"Fragments of a Tariff Discussion," c. December 1, 1847, reprinted in *Collected Works of Abraham Lincoln*, v. 1, p. 411. Rutgers University Press (1953, 1990).

*E*NEMIES

To correct the evils, great and small, which spring from want of sympathy, and from positive enmity, among *strangers*, as nations, or as individuals, is one of the highest functions of civilization.

"Address before the Wisconsin State Agricultural Society, Milwaukee, Wisconsin," September 30, 1859, reprinted in *Collected Works of Abraham Lincoln*, v. 3, p. 471. Rutgers University Press (1953, 1990).

*E*RRORS

I claim not to be more free from errors than others—perhaps scarcely so much....

"Speech at Springfield, Illinois," July 17, 1858, reprinted in *Collected Works of Abraham Lincoln*, v. 2, p. 512. Rutgers University Press (1953, 1990).

In my administration I might have committed some errors. It would be, indeed, remarkable if I had not. I have acted according to my best judgement in every case.

"Reply to Members of the Presbyterian General Assembly," June 2, 1863, reprinted in *Collected Works of Abraham Lincoln*, v. 6, p. 245. Rutgers University Press (1953, 1990).

*F*AILURE

The *probability* that we may fall in the struggle *ought not* to deter us from the support of a cause we believe to be just; it *shall not* deter me.

"Speech on the Sub-Treasury," December 26, 1839, reprinted in *Collected Works of Abraham Lincoln*, v. 1, p. 178. Rutgers University Press (1953, 1990).

I find quite as much material for a lecture in those points wherein I have failed, as in those wherein I have been moderately successful.

> Fragment: "Notes for a Law Lecture," [July 1, 1850?], reprinted in *Collected Works of Abraham Lincoln*, v. 2, p. 81. Rutgers University Press (1953, 1990).

I shall attend to it as well as I know how, which, G-d knows, will not be very well.

> Letter to Norman B. Judd, December 14, 1859, reprinted in *Collected Works of Abraham Lincoln*, v. 3, p. 509. Rutgers University Press (1953, 1990).

If I fail, it will be for lack of *ability,* and not of *purpose.*

> Letter to Joshua R. Giddings, June 26, 1860, reprinted in *Collected Works of Abraham Lincoln*, v. 4, p.81. Rutgers University Press (1953, 1990).

I know not how to aid you, save in the assurance of one of mature age, and much severe experience, that you *can* not fail, if you resolutely determine, that you *will* not.

> Letter to George C. Latham, July 22, 1860, reprinted in *Collected Works of Abraham Lincoln*, v. 4, p.87. Rutgers University Press (1953, 1990).
>
> To a young man rejected by a college.

In your temporary failure there is no evidence that you may not yet be a better scholar and a more successful man in the great struggle of life than many others who have entered college more easily.

> Letter to George C. Latham, July 22, 1860, reprinted in *Collected Works of Abraham Lincoln*, v. 4, p. 87. Rutgers University Press (1953, 1990).

Although you were not successful, the attempt was not an error. . . .

> "Congratulations to the Army of the Potomac," December 22, 1862, reprinted in *Collected Works of Abraham Lincoln*, v. 6, p. 13. Rutgers University Press (1953, 1990).

*F*AIR *PLAY*

Fair play is a jewel. Give him a chance if you can.

> Letter to Simon Cameron, August 10, 1861, reprinted in *Collected Works of Abraham Lincoln*, v. 4, p. 480. Rutgers University Press (1953, 1990).

*F*AREWELL TO HOME TOWN

My friends—No one, not in my situation, can appreciate my feeling of sadness at this parting. To this place, and the kindness of these people, I owe everything. Here I have lived a quarter of a century, and I have passed from a young to an old man. Here my children have been born, and one is buried. I now leave, not knowing when, or whether ever, I may return, with a task before me greater than that which rested upon Washington. Without the assistance of that Divine Being, who ever attended him, I cannot succeed. With that assistance I cannot fail. Trusting in Him, who can go with me, and remain with you and be everywhere for good, let us confidently hope that all will yet be well. To His care commending you, as I hope in your prayers you will commend me, I bid you an affectionate farewell.

"Farewell Address at Springfield, Illinois," February 11, 1861, reprinted in *Collected Works of Abraham Lincoln*, v. 4, p. 190. Rutgers University Press (1953, 1990).

*F*ARMERS AND FARMING

I believe it is also true that the soil has never been pushed up to one-half of its capacity.

"Address before the Wisconsin State Agricultural Society, Milwaukee, Wisconsin," September 30, 1859, reprinted in *Collected Works of Abraham Lincoln*, v. 3, p. 474. Rutgers University Press (1953, 1990).

I presume I am not expected to employ the time assigned me, in the mere flattery of the farmers, as a class. My opinion of them is that, in proportion to numbers, they are neither better nor worse than other people. . . . And I believe there really are more attempts at flattering them than any other. . . .

"Address before the Wisconsin State Agricultural Society, Milwaukee, Wisconsin," September 30, 1859, reprinted in *Collected Works of Abraham Lincoln*, v. 3, p. 472. Rutgers University Press (1953, 1990).

The ambition for broad acres leads to poor farming, even with men of energy.

"Address before the Wisconsin State Agricultural Society, Milwaukee, Wisconsin," September 30, 1859, reprinted in *Collected Works of Abraham Lincoln*, v. 3, p. 475. Rutgers University Press (1953, 1990).

*F*AVORS

No one has needed favors more than I, and generally, few have been less unwilling to accept them; but in this case, favor to me, would be injustice to the public, and therefore I must beg your pardon for declining it.

Letter to Robert Allen, June 21, 1836, reprinted in *Collected Works of Abraham Lincoln*, v. 1, p. 49. Rutgers University Press (1953, 1990).

Reply to politician who claimed to possess damaging information about Lincoln but was withholding it as a favor.

But I shall not ask any favors at all.

"Sixth Debate with Stephen A. Douglas, at Quincy, Illinois," October 13, 1858, reprinted in *Collected Works of Abraham Lincoln*, v. 3, p. 253. Rutgers University Press (1953, 1990).

I am never done asking for favors.

Letter to Jesse A. Pickrell, November 3, 1859, reprinted in *Collected Works of Abraham Lincoln*, v. 3, p. 493. Rutgers University Press (1953, 1990).

*F*EES OF LAWYERS

I will do my best for the "biggest kind of a fee" as you say, if we succeed, and nothing if we fail.

Letter to Samuel D. Marshall, November 11, 1842, reprinted in *Collected Works of Abraham Lincoln*, v. 1, p. 305. Rutgers University Press (1953, 1990).

Whatever fees we earn at a distance, if not paid *before*, we have noticed we never hear of after the work is done.

Letter to James S. Irwin, November 2, 1842, reprinted in *Collected Works of Abraham Lincoln*, v. 1, p. 304. Rutgers University Press (1953, 1990).

The matter of fees is important, far beyond the mere question of bread and butter involved. Properly attended to, fuller justice is done to both lawyer and client.

Fragment: "Notes for a Law Lecture," [July 1, 1850?], reprinted in *Collected Works of Abraham Lincoln*, v. 2, p. 82. Rutgers University Press (1953, 1990).

I can not tell in advance what fee I would charge, because I can not know the amount of trouble I may have.

> Letter to Thomas Meharry, April 21, 1857, reprinted in *Collected Works of Abraham Lincoln*, v. 2, p. 394. Rutgers University Press (1953, 1990).

Are, or not the *amount* of *labor*, the *doubtfulness* and *difficulty* of the *question*, the *degree* of *success* in the *result*; and the *amount* of pecuniary interest *involved*, not merely in the particular case, but covered by the principle decided, and thereby *secured* to the client, all proper elements by the custom of the profession to consider in determining what is a reasonable fee in a given case.

> "Brief of Argument," [June 23, 1857], reprinted in *Collected Works of Abraham Lincoln*, v. 2, p. 398. Rutgers University Press (1953, 1990).

> See also LAWYERS.

*F*OOLS

A fellow once advertised that he had made a discovery by which he could make a new man out of an old one, and have enough of the stuff left to make a little yellow dog.

> "Speech in the U.S. House of Representatives on the Presidential Question," July 27, 1848, reprinted in *Collected Works of Abraham Lincoln*, v. 1, p. 508. Rutgers University Press (1953, 1990).

> See also LIES.

*F*ORGIVENESS

I am a patient man—always willing to forgive on the Christian terms of repentance; and also to give ample *time* for repentance.

> Letter to Reverdy Johnson, July 26, 1862, reprinted in *Collected Works of Abraham Lincoln*, v. 5, p. 343. Rutgers University Press (1953, 1990).

On principle I dislike an oath which requires a man to swear he *has* not done wrong. It rejects the Christian principle of forgiveness on terms of repentance. I think it is enough if the man does no wrong *hereafter*.

> Letter to Edwin M. Stanton, February 5, 1864, reprinted in *Collected Works of Abraham Lincoln*, v. 7, p. 169. Rutgers University Press (1953, 1990).

*F*OUNDERS *OF THE UNITED STATES*

If they succeeded, they were to be immortalized; their names were to be transferred to counties and cities, and rivers and mountains; and to be revered and sung, and toasted through all time.

"Lyceum Address," Springfield, Illinois, January 27, 1838, reprinted in *Collected Works of Abraham Lincoln*, v. 1, p. 113. Rutgers University Press (1953, 1990).

Four score and seven years ago our fathers brought forth on this continent, a new nation, conceived in Liberty, and dedicated to the proposition that all men are created equal.

"Gettysburg Address," November 19, 1863, reprinted in *Collected Works of Abraham Lincoln*, v. 7, p. 23. Rutgers University Press (1953, 1990).

*F*REEDOM

If destruction be our lot, we must ourselves be its author and finisher. As a nation of freemen, we must live through all time, or die by suicide.

"Lyceum Address," Springfield, Illinois, January 27, 1838, reprinted in *Collected Works of Abraham Lincoln*, v. 1, p. 109. Rutgers University Press (1953, 1990).

God-given rights to enjoy the fruits of their own labor. . . .

"Speech at Carlinville, Illinois," August 31, 1858, reprinted in *Collected Works of Abraham Lincoln*, v. 3, p. 81. Rutgers University Press (1953, 1990).

The universality of freedom. . . .

"Speech at Carlinville, Illinois," August 31, 1858, reprinted in *Collected Works of Abraham Lincoln*, v. 3, p. 81. Rutgers University Press (1953, 1990).

Familiarize yourself with the chains of bondage, and you are preparing your own limbs to wear them.

"Speech at Edwardsville, Illinois," September 11, 1858, reprinted in *Collected Works of Abraham Lincoln*, v. 3, p. 95. Rutgers University Press (1953, 1990).

I am for the people of the whole nation doing just as they please in all matters which concern the whole nation; for those of each part doing just as they choose in all matters which concern no other part; and for each individual doing just as he chooses in all matters which concern nobody else. This is the principle.

"Fragment of a Speech," [c. May 18, 1858], reprinted in *Collected Works of Abraham Lincoln*, v. 2, p. 452. Rutgers University Press (1953, 1990).

What constitutes the bulwark of our own liberty and independence? It is not our frowning battlements, our bristling sea coasts, the guns of our war steamers, or the strength of our gallant and disciplined army. These are not our reliance against a resumption of tyranny in our fair land. All of them may be turned against our liberties, without making us stronger or weaker for the struggle. Our reliance is in the *love of liberty* which God has planted in our bosoms.

"Speech at Edwardsville, Illinois," September 11, 1858, reprinted in *Collected Works of Abraham Lincoln*, v. 3, p. 95. Rutgers University Press (1953, 1990).

I have often inquired of myself, what great principle or idea it was that kept this Confederacy so long together. It was not the mere matter of the separation of the colonies from the mother land; but something in that Declaration [of Independence] giving liberty, not alone to the people of this country, but hope to the world for all future time. It was that which gave [the] promise that in due time the weights should be lifted from the shoulders of all men, and that *all* should have an equal chance.

"Speech in Independence Hall," Philadelphia, Pennsylvania, February 22, 1861, reprinted in *Collected Works of Abraham Lincoln*, v. 4, p. 240. Rutgers University Press (1953, 1990).

See also AMERICAN DREAM

In *giving* freedom to the *slave,* we *assure* freedom to the *free. . . .*

"Annual Message to Congress," December 1, 1862, reprinted in *Collected Works of Abraham Lincoln*, v. 5, p. 537. Rutgers University Press (1953, 1990).

The world has never had a good definition of the word liberty, and the American people, just now, are much in want of one. We all declare for liberty; but in using the same *word* we do not all mean the same *thing. . . .* The shepherd drives the wolf from the sheep's throat, for which the sheep thanks the shepherd as a *liberator*, while the wolf denounces him for the same act as the destroyer of liberty, especially as the sheep was a black one. Plainly the sheep and the wolf are not agreed upon a definition of the word liberty; and precisely the same difference prevails today among us human creatures. . . .

"Address at Sanitary Fair," Baltimore, Maryland, April 18, 1864, reprinted in *Collected Works of Abraham Lincoln*, v. 7, p. 301. Rutgers University Press (1953, 1990).

*F*REMONT, *GENERAL JOHN C.*

He is losing the confidence of men near him, whose support any man
in his position must have to be successful. His cardinal mistake is that he
isolates himself, and allows nobody to see him; and by which he does not
know what is going on in the very matter he is dealing with.

Letter to David Hunter, September 9, 1861, reprinted in *Collected Works of Abraham Lincoln*, v. 4,
p. 513. Rutgers University Press (1953, 1990).

*F*RIENDS

How miserably things seem to be arranged in this world. If we have no
friends, we have no pleasure; and if we have them, we are sure to lose them,
and be doubly pained by the loss.

Letter to Joshua F. Speed, February 25, 1842, reprinted in *Collected Works of Abraham Lincoln*, v. 1,
p. 281. Rutgers University Press (1953, 1990).

The friends I left that parting day,
    How changed, as time has sped!
Young childhood grown, strong manhood gray,
    And half of all are dead.

"My Childhood Home I See Again," c. April, 1846, reprinted in *Collected Works of Abraham Lincoln*,
v. 1, p. 379. Rutgers University Press (1953, 1990).

It is a delicate matter to oppose the wishes of a friend. . . .

Letter to William B. Preston, May 16, 1849, reprinted in *Collected Works of Abraham Lincoln*, v. 2, p. 48.
Rutgers University Press (1953, 1990).

The better part of one's life consists of his friendships. . . .

Letter to Joseph Gillespie, July 13, 1849, reprinted in *Collected Works of Abraham Lincoln*, v. 2, p. 57.
Rutgers University Press (1953, 1990).

We must never sell old friends to buy old enemies.

Letter to Ozias M. Hatch, March 24, 1858, reprinted in *Collected Works of Abraham Lincoln, Supplement
1832–1865*, v. 10, p. 29. Rutgers University Press (1953, 1990).

I wish to assure you as once a friend and still, I hope, not an enemy. . . .

Letter to Alexander H. Stephens, December 22, 1860, reprinted in *Collected Works of Abraham Lincoln*,
v. 4, p. 160. Rutgers University Press (1953, 1990).

Written to the future Vice President of the Confederacy.

The loss of enemies does not compensate for the loss of friends.

> Letter to William H. Seward, June 30, 1862, reprinted in *Collected Works of Abraham Lincoln*, v. 5, p. 295. Rutgers University Press (1953, 1990).
>
> On the loss of troops in battle.

I distrust the *wisdom* if not the *sincerity* of friends, who would hold my hands while my enemies stab me.

> Letter to Reverdy Johnson, July 26, 1862, reprinted in *Collected Works of Abraham Lincoln*, v. 5, p. 343. Rutgers University Press (1953, 1990).

*F*UTURE

Few can be induced to labor exclusively for posterity; and none will do it enthusiastically.

> "Temperance Address," February 22, 1842, reprinted in *Collected Works of Abraham Lincoln*, v. 1, p. 275. Rutgers University Press (1953, 1990).

If we could first know *where* we are, and *whither* we are tending, we could then better judge *what* to do, and *how* to do it.

> "A House Divided," speech at Springfield, Illinois, June 16, 1858, reprinted in *Collected Works of Abraham Lincoln*, v. 2, p. 461. Rutgers University Press (1953, 1990).

The struggle of today, is not altogether for today—it is for a vast future also.

> "Annual Message to Congress," December 3, 1861, reprinted in *Collected Works of Abraham Lincoln*, v. 5, p. 53. Rutgers University Press (1953, 1990).

In any future great national trial, compared with the men of this, we shall have as weak, and as strong; as silly and as wise; as bad and good.

> "Response to a Serenade," November 10, 1864, reprinted in *Collected Works of Abraham Lincoln*, v. 8, p. 101. Rutgers University Press (1953, 1990).

*G*AMBLERS

They constitute a portion of the population, that is worse than useless. . . .

> "Lyceum Address," Springfield, Illinois, January 27, 1838, reprinted in *Collected Works of Abraham Lincoln*, v. 1, p. 110. Rutgers University Press (1953, 1990).

GENERALS

Now, what right had a brigadier general, when approaching the enemy's position, and directly under his fire, to sink down and roll over in a deep slimy canal and struggle there before he got out, how long, another brigadier general cannot tell, when the whole of both their brigades got across that same "slimy canal," without any difficulty worth mentioning?

"Speech to the Springfield Scott Club," August 26, 1852, reprinted in *Collected Works of Abraham Lincoln*, v. 2, p. 149. Rutgers University Press (1953, 1990).

The difference between one who *is* a general, and one who is *called* a general. . . .

"Speech to the Springfield Scott Club," August 26, 1852, reprinted in *Collected Works of Abraham Lincoln*, v. 2, p. 148. Rutgers University Press (1953, 1990).

It has been said that one bad general is better than two good ones; and the saying is true, if taken to mean no more than that an army is better directed by a single mind, though inferior, than by two superior ones, at variance, and cross purposes with each other.

"Annual Message to Congress," December 3, 1861, reprinted in *Collected Works of Abraham Lincoln*, v. 5, p. 51. Rutgers University Press (1953, 1990).

Major Generalships in the Regular Army are not as plenty as blackberries.

Letter to Richard Yates and William Butler, April 10, 1862, reprinted in *Collected Works of Abraham Lincoln*, v. 5, p. 186. Rutgers University Press (1953, 1990).

GENTLEMEN

I set out in this campaign, with the intention of conducting it strictly as a gentleman, in substance at least, if not in the outside polish. The latter I shall never be.

"Speech at Springfield, Illinois," July 17, 1858, reprinted in *Collected Works of Abraham Lincoln*, v. 2, p. 513. Rutgers University Press (1953, 1990).

GETTYSBURG ADDRESS

Four score and seven years ago our fathers brought forth on this continent, a new nation, conceived in Liberty, and dedicated to the proposition that all men are created equal.

Now we are engaged in a great civil war, testing whether that nation, or any nation so conceived and so dedicated, can long endure. We are met on a great battlefield of that war. We have come to dedicate a portion of that field, as a final resting place for those who here gave their lives that that nation might live. It is altogether fitting and proper that we should do this.

But, in a larger sense, we can not dedicate—we can not consecrate—we can not hallow—this ground. The brave men, living and dead, who struggled here, have consecrated it, far above our poor power to add or detract. The world will little note, nor long remember what we say here, but it can never forget what they did here. It is for us the living, rather, to be dedicated here to the unfinished work which they who fought here have thus far so nobly advanced. It is rather for us to be here dedicated to the great task remaining before us—that from these honored dead we take increased devotion to that cause for which they gave the last full measure of devotion—that we here highly resolve that these dead shall not have died in vain—that this nation, under God, shall have a new birth of freedom—and that government of the people, by the people, for the people, shall not perish from the earth.

"Gettysburg Address," November 19, 1863, reprinted in *Collected Works of Abraham Lincoln*, v. 7, p. 23. Rutgers University Press (1953, 1990).

I am pleased to know that, in your judgment, the little I did say was not entirely a failure.

Letter to Edward Everett, November 20, 1863, reprinted in *Collected Works of Abraham Lincoln*, v. 7, p. 24. Rutgers University Press (1953, 1990).

GETTYSBURG CAMPAIGN'S CONCLUSION

We have certain information that Vicksburg surrendered to General Grant on the 4th of July. Now, if General Meade can complete his work, so gloriously prosecuted thus far, by the literal or substantial destruction of Lee's army, the rebellion will be over.

Letter to General Henry W. Halleck, July 7, 1863, reprinted in *Collected Works of Abraham Lincoln*, v. 6, p. 319. Rutgers University Press (1953, 1990).

I do not believe you appreciate the magnitude of the misfortune involved in Lee's escape. He was within your easy grasp, and to have closed upon him would, in connection with our other late successes, have ended the war. As it is, the war will be prolonged indefinitely.... Your golden opportunity is gone, and I am distressed immeasurably because of it.

> Unsent letter to General George G. Meade, July 14, 1863, reprinted in *Collected Works of Abraham Lincoln*, v. 6, p. 328. Rutgers University Press (1953, 1990).

GINGERBREAD

He said he reckoned he loved it better than any other man, and got less of it.

> "First Debate with Stephen A. Douglas at Ottawa, Illinois," August 21, 1858, reprinted in *Collected Works of Abraham Lincoln*, v. 3, p. 20. Rutgers University Press (1953, 1990).

GOD

He renders the worst of human conditions tolerable, while He permits the best to be nothing better than tolerable.

> Letter to Mary Speed, September 27, 1841, reprinted in *Collected Works of Abraham Lincoln*, v. 1, p. 260. Rutgers University Press (1953, 1990).

He notes the fall of a sparrow and numbers the hairs of our heads, and He will not forget the dying man who puts his trust in Him.

> Letter to John D. Johnston, January 12, 1851, reprinted in *Collected Works of Abraham Lincoln*, v. 2, p. 97. Rutgers University Press (1953, 1990).

There is no contending against the Will of God; but still there is some difficulty in ascertaining, and applying it, to particular cases.

> "Fragment on Pro-slavery Theology," [October 1, 1858?], reprinted in *Collected Works of Abraham Lincoln*, v. 3, p. 204. Rutgers University Press (1953, 1990).

In great contests each party claims to act in accordance with the will of God. Both *may* be, and one *must* be, wrong. God can not be *for* and *against* the same thing at the same time.

> "Meditation on the Divine Will," [September 2, 1862?], reprinted in *Collected Works of Abraham Lincoln*, v. 5, p. 403. Rutgers University Press (1953, 1990).

The will of God prevails.

> "Meditation on the Divine Will," [September 2, 1862?], reprinted in *Collected Works of Abraham Lincoln*, v. 5, p. 403. Rutgers University Press (1953, 1990).

I hope it will not be irreverent for me to say that if it is probable that God would reveal his will to others, on a point so connected with my duty [emancipation], it might be supposed he would reveal it directly to me. . . .

"Reply to Chicago Christians," September 13, 1862, reprinted in *Collected Works of Abraham Lincoln*, v. 5, p. 419. Rutgers University Press (1953, 1990).

Reply to delegation claiming God wanted emancipation.

GOOD AND EVIL

By the *fruit* the tree is to be known. An *evil* tree can not bring forth *good* fruit.

Letter to Williamson Durley, October 3, 1845, reprinted in *Collected Works of Abraham Lincoln*, v. 1, p. 347. Rutgers University Press (1953, 1990).

The true rule, in determining to embrace, or reject any thing, is not whether it have any evil in it; but whether it have more of evil, than of good. There are few things *wholly* evil, or *wholly* good.

"Speech in United States House of Representatives on Internal Improvements," June 20, 1848, reprinted in *Collected Works of Abraham Lincoln*, v. 1, p. 484. Rutgers University Press (1953, 1990).

GOVERNMENT

The legitimate object of government, is to do for a community of people, whatever they need to have done, but can not do, *at all*, or can not, *so well do*, for themselves—in their separate, and individual capacities.

"Fragment on Government," [July 1, 1854?], reprinted in *Collected Works of Abraham Lincoln*, v. 2, p. 220. Rutgers University Press (1953, 1990).

According to our ancient faith, the just powers of governments are derived from the consent of the governed.

"Speech at Peoria, Illinois," October 16, 1854, reprinted in *Collected Works of Abraham Lincoln*, v. 2, p. 266. Rutgers University Press (1953, 1990).

In all that the people can individually do as well for themselves, government ought not to interfere.

"Fragment on Government," [July 1, 1854?], reprinted in *Collected Works of Abraham Lincoln*, v. 2, p. 220. Rutgers University Press (1953, 1990).

The best framed and best administered governments are necessarily expensive; while by errors in frame and maladministration most of them are more onerous than they need be, and some of them very oppressive.

"Fragment on Government," [July 1, 1854?], reprinted in *Collected Works of Abraham Lincoln*, v. 2, p. 221. Rutgers University Press (1953, 1990).

This government was instituted to secure the blessings of freedom. . . .

"Speech at Edwardsvillle, Illinois," September 11, 1858, reprinted in *Collected Works of Abraham Lincoln*, v. 3, p. 92. Rutgers University Press (1953, 1990).

Working men are the basis of all governments, for the plain reason that they are the most numerous. . . .

"Speech to Germans" at Cincinnati, Ohio, February 12, 1861, reprinted in *Collected Works of Abraham Lincoln*, v. 4, p. 202. Rutgers University Press (1953, 1990).

I know the American People are *much* attached to their Government; I know they would suffer *much* for its sake. . . .

"Lyceum Address," Springfield, Illinois, January 27, 1838, reprinted in *Collected Works of Abraham Lincoln*, v. 1, p. 112. Rutgers University Press (1953, 1990).

The people will save their government, if the government itself will do its part only indifferently well.

"Message to Congress in Special Session," July 4, 1861, reprinted in *Collected Works of Abraham Lincoln*, v. 4, p. 432. Rutgers University Press (1953, 1990).

Government is not charged with the duty of redressing, or preventing, all the wrongs in the world.

"Notes for Speeches at Columbus and Cincinnati, Ohio," [September 16-17, 1859], reprinted in *Collected Works of Abraham Lincoln*, v. 3, p. 435. Rutgers University Press (1953, 1990).

Government should not act for revenge.

Letter to Edwin M. Stanton, May 17, 1864, reprinted in *Collected Works of Abraham Lincoln*, v. 7, p. 345. Rutgers University Press (1953, 1990).

We should avoid planting and cultivating too many thorns in the bosom of society.

Letter to Edwin M. Stanton, March 18, 1864, reprinted in *Collected Works of Abraham Lincoln*, v. 7, p. 255. Rutgers University Press (1953, 1990).

GOVERNMENT IN WAR

In using the strong hand, as now compelled to do, the government has a difficult duty to perform. At the very best, it will by turns do both too little and too much.

Letter to Edwin M. Stanton, March 18, 1864, reprinted in *Collected Works of Abraham Lincoln*, v. 7, p. 255. Rutgers University Press (1953, 1990).

It has long been a grave question whether any government, not *too* strong for the liberties of its people, can be strong *enough* to maintain its own existence, in great emergencies.

"Response to a Serenade," November 10, 1864, reprinted in *Collected Works of Abraham Lincoln*, v. 8, p. 100. Rutgers University Press (1953, 1990).

GRANT, ULYSSES S.

General Grant is a copious worker, and fighter, but a very meager writer, or telegrapher.

Letter to Ambrose E. Burnside, July 27, 1863, reprinted in *Collected Works of Abraham Lincoln*, v. 6, p. 350. Rutgers University Press (1953, 1990).

The almost inestimable service you have done the country.

Letter to General Ulysses S. Grant, July 13, 1863, reprinted in *Collected Works of Abraham Lincoln*, v. 6, p. 326. Rutgers University Press (1953, 1990).

On the capture of Vicksburg.

I wish to express, in this way, my entire satisfaction with what you have done up to this time, so far as I understand it. The particulars of your plans I neither know, or seek to know. You are vigilant and self-reliant; and, pleased with this, I wish not to obtrude any constraints or restraints upon you. . . . If there is anything wanting which is within my power to give, do not fail to let me know it.

Letter to General Ulysses S. Grant, April 30, 1864, reprinted in *Collected Works of Abraham Lincoln*, v. 7, p. 324. Rutgers University Press (1953, 1990).

GREED

It is as if two starving men had divided their only loaf; the one had hastily swallowed his half, and then grabbed the other half just as he was putting it to his mouth!

"Speech at Peoria, Illinois," October 16, 1854, reprinted in *Collected Works of Abraham Lincoln*, v. 2, p. 262. Rutgers University Press (1953, 1990).

If pecuniary greed can be made to aid us in such effort, let us be thankful that so much good can be got out of pecuniary greed.

Letter to Edward R. S. Canby, December 12, 1864, reprinted in *Collected Works of Abraham Lincoln*, v. 8, p. 164. Rutgers University Press (1953, 1990).

About trading in cotton and saving the Union.

HANDWRITING

His cursed, unreadable, and ungodly handwriting.

Letter to William H. Herndon, January 19, 1848, reprinted in *Collected Works of Abraham Lincoln*, v. 1, p. 445. Rutgers University Press (1953, 1990).

On Louis W. Chandler.

HASTE

Make haste slowly.

Letter to Francis H. Peirpont, March 20, 1862, reprinted in *Collected Works of Abraham Lincoln*, v. 5, p. 166. Rutgers University Press (1953, 1990).

Beware of rashness. Beware of rashness, but with energy, and sleepless vigilance, go forward, and give us victories.

Letter to General Joseph Hooker, January 26, 1863, reprinted in *Collected Works of Abraham Lincoln*, v. 6, p. 79. Rutgers University Press (1953, 1990).

Hearts

But who is to be the judge of hearts. . . ?

> Letter to Carl Schurz, November 24, 1862, reprinted in *Collected Works of Abraham Lincoln*, v. 5, p. 509. Rutgers University Press (1953, 1990).

Heaven

"Better lay down that spade you're stealing, Paddy,—if you don't you'll pay for it at the day of judgement." "By the powers, if ye'll credit me so long, I'll take another, jist."

> "Temperance Address," February 22, 1842, reprinted in *Collected Works of Abraham Lincoln*, v. 1, p. 276. Rutgers University Press (1953, 1990).

There is something so ludicrous in *promises* of good, or *threats* of evil, a great way off, as to render the whole subject with which they are connected, easily turned into ridicule.

> "Temperance Address," February 22, 1842, reprinted in *Collected Works of Abraham Lincoln*, v. 1, p. 275. Rutgers University Press (1953, 1990).

You say you would almost give your place in Heaven for $70 or $80. Then you value your place in Heaven very cheaply. . . .

> Letter to Thomas Lincoln and John D. Johnston, December 24, 1848, reprinted in *Collected Works of Abraham Lincoln*, v. 2, p. 16. Rutgers University Press (1953, 1990).

Helping people

It is a cheering thought throughout life that something can be done to ameliorate the condition of those who have been subject to the hard usage of the world.

> "Address on Colonization to a Deputation of Negroes," August 14, 1862, reprinted in *Collected Works of Abraham Lincoln*, v. 5, p. 373. Rutgers University Press (1953, 1990).

History

A *living history* was to be found in every family. . . .

> "Lyceum Address," Springfield, Illinois, January 27, 1838, reprinted in *Collected Works of Abraham Lincoln*, v. 1, p. 115. Rutgers University Press (1953, 1990).
>
> Referring to the people of the American Revolution.

But *those* histories are gone. They *can* be read no more forever. They *were* a fortress of strength; but, what invading foemen could *never do*, the silent artillery of time *has done*; the leveling of its walls. They are gone.

"Lyceum Address," Springfield, Illinois, January 27, 1838, reprinted in *Collected Works of Abraham Lincoln*, v. 1, p. 115. Rutgers University Press (1953, 1990).

What has once happened, will invariably happen again, when the same circumstances which combined to produce it, shall again combine in the same way.

"Speech on the Sub-Treasury," December 26, 1839, reprinted in *Collected Works of Abraham Lincoln*, v. 1, p. 165. Rutgers University Press (1953, 1990).

History is philosophy teaching by example. . . .

"Speech to the Springfield Scott Club," August 26, 1852, reprinted in *Collected Works of Abraham Lincoln*, v. 2, p. 148. Rutgers University Press (1953, 1990).

The foregoing history may not be precisely accurate in every particular; but I am sure it is sufficiently so, for all the uses I shall attempt to make of it. . . .

"Speech at Peoria, Illinois," October 16, 1854, reprinted in *Collected Works of Abraham Lincoln*, v. 2, p. 254. Rutgers University Press (1953, 1990).

This flat contradiction of the known history of the country.

"Speech at Peoria, Illinois," October 16, 1854, reprinted in *Collected Works of Abraham Lincoln*, v. 2, p. 277. Rutgers University Press (1953, 1990).

On Senator Douglas's version of the history of slavery in Illinois.

We cannot escape history.

"Annual Message to Congress," December 1, 1862, reprinted in *Collected Works of Abraham Lincoln*, v. 5, p. 537. Rutgers University Press (1953, 1990).

I claim not to have controlled events, but confess plainly that events have controlled me.

Letter to Albert G. Hodges, April 4, 1864, reprinted in *Collected Works of Abraham Lincoln*, v. 7, p. 282. Rutgers University Press (1953, 1990).

*H*ONESTY

In very truth he was, the noblest work of God—an honest man.

"Eulogy on Benjamin Ferguson," February 8, 1842, reprinted in *Collected Works of Abraham Lincoln*, v. 1, p. 269. Rutgers University Press (1953, 1990).

No men living are more worthy to be trusted than those who toil up from poverty—none less inclined to take, or touch, aught which they have not honestly earned.

"Annual Message to Congress," December 3, 1861, reprinted in *Collected Works of Abraham Lincoln*, v. 5, p. 52. Rutgers University Press (1953, 1990).

The writer's word is good to the utmost hair's-breadth for what he says.

Letter to Edwin M. Stanton, April 15, 1862, reprinted in *Collected Works of Abraham Lincoln*, v. 5, p. 191. Rutgers University Press (1953, 1990).

Seconding opinion about Major Robert Allen, quartermaster.

$\mathcal{H}$ONOR

The fiery trial through which we pass, will light us down, in honor or dishonor, to the latest generation.

"Annual Message to Congress," December 1, 1862, reprinted in *Collected Works of Abraham Lincoln*, v. 5, p. 537. Rutgers University Press (1953, 1990).

$\mathcal{H}$OPE

They teach *hope* to all—*despair* to none.

"Temperance Address," February 22, 1842, reprinted in *Collected Works of Abraham Lincoln*, v. 1, p. 276. Rutgers University Press (1953, 1990).

On reformed alcoholics.

The power of hope upon human exertion, and happiness, is wonderful.

"Fragment on Free Labor," [September 17, 1859?], reprinted in *Collected Works of Abraham Lincoln*, v. 3, p. 462. Rutgers University Press (1953, 1990).

This expression of hope, however, must not be construed into a promise.

Letter to Joel Parker, July 25, 1863, reprinted in *Collected Works of Abraham Lincoln*, v. 6, p. 348. Rutgers University Press (1953, 1990).

*H*OUSE DIVIDED

Welcome, or unwelcome, agreeable, or disagreeable, whether this shall be an entire slave nation, *is* the issue before us.

"Fragment of a Speech," [c. May 18, 1858], reprinted in *Collected Works of Abraham Lincoln*, v. 2, p. 453. Rutgers University Press (1953, 1990).

"A house divided against itself cannot stand."
I believe this government cannot endure, permanently half *slave* and half *free*.
I do not expect the Union to be *dissolved*—I do not expect the house to *fall*—but I *do* expect it will cease to be divided.
It will become *all* one thing, or *all* the other.

"A House Divided," speech at Springfield, Illinois, June 16, 1858, reprinted in *Collected Works of Abraham Lincoln*, v. 2, p. 461. Rutgers University Press (1953, 1990).

*H*UMAN CONDITION

How true it is that "God tempers the wind to the shorn lamb," or in other words, that He renders the worst of human conditions tolerable, while He permits the best to be nothing better than tolerable.

Letter to Mary Speed, September 27, 1841, reprinted in *Collected Works of Abraham Lincoln*, v. 1, p. 260. Rutgers University Press (1953, 1990).

Based on a French proverb.

*H*UMAN DUTY

I hold that while man exists, it is his duty to improve not only his own condition, but to assist in ameliorating mankind; and therefore, . . . I am for those means which will give the greatest good to the greatest number.

"Speech to Germans" at Cincinnati, Ohio, February 12, 1861, reprinted in *Collected Works of Abraham Lincoln*, v. 4, p. 202. Rutgers University Press (1953, 1990).

HUMAN NATURE

It is not much in the nature of man to be driven to any thing. . . .

"Temperance Address," February 22, 1842, reprinted in *Collected Works of Abraham Lincoln*, v. 1, p. 272. Rutgers University Press (1953, 1990).

Human nature will not change.

"Response to a Serenade," November 10, 1864, reprinted in *Collected Works of Abraham Lincoln*, v. 8, p. 101. Rutgers University Press (1953, 1990).

HUMANITY

Man, from the first, was to dig out his destiny.

"First Lecture on Discoveries and Inventions," April 6, 1858, reprinted in *Collected Works of Abraham Lincoln*, v. 2, p. 437. Rutgers University Press (1953, 1990).

All good, intelligent people are very much alike.

Letter to William Gooding, April 6, 1860, reprinted in *Collected Works of Abraham Lincoln*, v. 4, p. 36. Rutgers University Press (1953, 1990).

HUSBANDS AND WIVES

As an old friend said. . . . When he lost his first wife, who had been a great help to him in his business, he thought he was ruined—that he could never find another to fill her place. At length, however, he married another, who he found did quite as well as the first, and that his opinion now was that any woman would do well who was well done by.

"Remarks at Bloomington, Illinois," November 21, 1860, reprinted in *Collected Works of Abraham Lincoln*, v. 4, p. 143. Rutgers University Press (1953, 1990).

As the fisherman's wife, whose drowned husband was brought home with his body full of eels, said when she was asked, "What was to be done with him?" *"Take the eels out and set him again."*

"Fifth Debate with Stephen A. Douglas, at Galesburg, Illinois," October 7, 1858, reprinted in *Collected Works of Abraham Lincoln*, v. 3, p. 228. Rutgers University Press (1953, 1990).

All I can say now is to recommend . . . to prosecute the war against one another in the most vigorous manner. I say to them again— "Go it, husband!— Go it, bear!"

"Seventh and Last Debate with Stephen A. Douglas at Alton, Illinois," October 15, 1858, reprinted in *Collected Works of Abraham Lincoln*, v. 3, p. 298. Rutgers University Press (1953, 1990).

On Democratic Party infighting. See also MARRIAGE

*I*DLENESS

Vastly important to you, and still more so to your children that you should break this habit [of uselessly wasting time]. It is more important to them, because they have longer to live, and can keep out of an idle habit before they are in it; easier than they can get out after they are in.

Letter to Thomas Lincoln and John D. Johnston, December 24, 1848, reprinted in *Collected Works of Abraham Lincoln*, v. 2, p. 16. Rutgers University Press (1953, 1990).

*I*MMIGRANTS

I am not a Know-Nothing [anti-immigrant]. That is certain. How could I be? How can any one who abhors the oppression of negroes, be in favor of degrading classes of white people?

Letter to Joshua F. Speed, August 24, 1855, reprinted in *Collected Works of Abraham Lincoln*, v. 2, p. 323. Rutgers University Press (1953, 1990).

In regard to Germans and foreigners, I esteem foreigners no better than other people, nor any worse. They are all of the great family of men. . . .

"Speech to Germans" at Cincinnati, Ohio, February 12, 1861, reprinted in *Collected Works of Abraham Lincoln*, v. 4, p. 203. Rutgers University Press (1953, 1990).

*I*NAUGURAL ADDRESS, SECOND

At this second appearing to take the oath of the presidential office, there is less occasion for an extended address than there was at the first. Then a statement, somewhat in detail, of a course to be pursued, seemed fitting and proper. Now, at the expiration of four years, during which public declarations have been constantly called forth on every point and phase of the great contest which still absorbs the attention, and engrosses the energies of the nation, little that is new could be presented. The progress of our arms, upon which all else chiefly depends, is as well known to the public as to myself; and it is, I trust, reasonably satisfactory and encouraging to all. With high hope for the future, no prediction in regard to it is ventured.

On the occasion corresponding to this four years ago, all thoughts were anxiously directed to an impending civil-war. All dreaded it—all sought to avert it. While the inaugural address was being delivered from this place, devoted altogether to *saving* the Union without war, insurgent agents were in the city seeking to *destroy* it without war—seeking to dissolve the Union, and divide effects, by negotiation. Both parties deprecated war; but one of them would *make* war rather than let the nation survive; and the other would *accept* war rather than let it perish. And the war came.

One eighth of the whole population were colored slaves, not distributed generally over the Union, but localized in the Southern part of it. These slaves constituted a peculiar and powerful interest. All knew that this interest was, somehow, the cause of the war. To strengthen, perpetuate, and extend this interest was the object for which the insurgents would rend the Union, even by war; while the government claimed no right to do more than to restrict the territorial enlargement of it. Neither party expected for the war, the magnitude, or the duration, which it has already attained. Neither anticipated that the *cause* of the conflict might cease with, or even before, the conflict itself should cease. Each looked for an easier triumph, and a result less fundamental and astounding. Both read the same Bible, and pray to the same God; and each invokes His aid against the other. It may seem strange that any men should dare to ask a just God's assistance in wringing their bread from the sweat of other men's faces; but let us judge not that we be not judged. The prayers of both could not be answered; that of neither has been answered fully. The Almighty has His own purposes. "Woe unto the world because of offences! for it must needs be that offences come; but woe to that man by whom the offense cometh!" If we shall suppose that American Slavery is one of those offences which, in the providence of God, must needs come, but which, having continued through His appointed time, He now wills to remove, and that He gives to both North and South, this terrible war, as the woe due to those by whom the offence came, shall we discern therein any departure from those divine attributes which the believers in a Living God always ascribe to Him? Fondly do we hope— fervently do we pray—that this mighty scourge of war may speedily pass away. Yet, if God wills that it continue, until all the wealth piled by the bond-man's two hundred and fifty years of unrequited toil shall be sunk, and until every drop of blood drawn with the lash, shall be paid by another drawn with the sword, as was said three thousand years ago, so still it must be said "the judgments of the Lord, are true and righteous altogether"

With malice toward none; with charity for all; with firmness in the right, as God gives us to see the right, let us strive on to finish the work we are in; to bind up the nation's wounds; to care for him who shall have borne the battle, and for his widow, and his orphan—to do all which may achieve and cherish a just, and a lasting peace, among ourselves, and with all nations.

"Second Inaugural Address," March 4, 1865, reprinted in *Collected Works of Abraham Lincoln*, v. 8, p. 332. Rutgers University Press (1953, 1990).

*I*NEQUALITY

Inequality is certainly never to be embraced for it's own sake; but is every good thing to be discarded, which may be inseparably connected with some degree of it?

"Speech in United States House of Representatives on Internal Improvements," June 20, 1848, reprinted in *Collected Works of Abraham Lincoln*, v. 1, p. 484. Rutgers University Press (1953, 1990).

The [pernicious] principle . . . that no one shall have any, for fear all shall not have some.

"Discussion in Illinois Legislature," February 6, 1841, reprinted in *Collected Works of Abraham Lincoln*, v. 1, p. 233. Rutgers University Press (1953, 1990).

If the nation refuse to make improvements, of the more general kind, because their benefits may be somewhat local, a state may, for the same reason, refuse to make an improvement of a local kind, because its benefit may be somewhat general. . . . If this argument of "inequality" is sufficient any where, it is sufficient every where; and puts an end to improvements altogether.

"Speech in the United States House of Representatives on Internal Improvements," June 20, 1848, reprinted in *Collected Works of Abraham Lincoln*, v. 1, p. 484. Rutgers University Press (1953, 1990).

This capital [of the U.S.] is built at the public expense, for the public benefit; but does any one doubt that it is of some peculiar local advantage to the property holders, and business people of Washington? Shall we remove it for this reason? and if so, where shall we set it down, and be free from the difficulty?

"Speech in the United States House of Representatives on Internal Improvements," June 20, 1848, reprinted in *Collected Works of Abraham Lincoln*, v. 1, p. 484. Rutgers University Press (1953, 1990).

The great mass of [medieval] men . . . were utterly unconscious, that their *conditions*, or their *minds* were capable of improvement. They not only looked upon the educated few as superior beings; but they supposed themselves to be naturally incapable of rising to equality.

"Second Lecture on Discoveries and Inventions," February 11, 1859, reprinted in *Collected Works of Abraham Lincoln*, v. 3, p. 362. Rutgers University Press (1953, 1990).

*I*NSANITY

And when at length, tho' drear and long,
    Time soothed thy fiercer woes,
How plaintively thy mournful song
    Upon the still night rose.

I've heard it oft, as if I dreamed,
    Far distant, sweet, and lone—
The funeral dirge, it ever seemed
    Of reason dead and gone.

To drink its strains, I've stole away,
    All stealthily and still,
Ere yet the rising God of day
    Had streaked the Eastern hill.

Air held his breath; trees, with the spell,
    Seemed sorrowing angels round,
Whose swelling tears in dew-drops fell
    Upon the listening ground.

"The Maniac," c. September 6, 1846, reprinted in *Collected Works of Abraham Lincoln*, v. 1, p. 385. Rutgers University Press (1953, 1990).

But here's an object more of dread
    Than ought the grave contains—
A human form with reason fled,
    While wretched life remains.

"The Maniac," c. September 6, 1846, reprinted in *Collected Works of Abraham Lincoln*, v. 1, p. 385. Rutgers University Press (1953, 1990).

*I*NTENTIONS *AND* RESULTS

When I propose a certain measure of policy, it is not enough for me that I do not intend anything evil in the result, but it is incumbent on me to show that it has not a *tendency* to that result.

"Seventh and Last Debate with Stephen A. Douglas at Alton, Illinois," October 15, 1858, reprinted in *Collected Works of Abraham Lincoln*, v. 3, p. 308. Rutgers University Press (1953, 1990).

*I*NVITATION

You are to make our house your home. . . .

Letter to Norman B. Judd, August 3, 1860, reprinted in *Collected Works of Abraham Lincoln, Supplement 1832–1865*, v. 10, p. 58. Rutgers University Press (1953, 1990).

*J*EALOUSY

Suspicion and jealousy never did help any man in any situation.

Letter to William H. Herndon, July 10, 1848, reprinted in *Collected Works of Abraham Lincoln*, v. 1, p. 497. Rutgers University Press (1953, 1990).

*J*EFFERSON, THOMAS

Was, is, and perhaps will continue to be, the most distinguished politician of our history.

"Speech at Peoria, Illinois," October 16, 1854, reprinted in *Collected Works of Abraham Lincoln*, v. 2, p. 249. Rutgers University Press (1953, 1990).

*J*UDGMENT

I am compelled to take a more impartial and unprejudiced view of things. Without claiming to be your superior, which I do not, my position enables me to understand. . . .

Letter to Congressman Isaac N. Arnold, May 21, 1863, reprinted in *Collected Works of Abraham Lincoln*, v. 6, p. 231. Rutgers University Press (1953, 1990).

JURIES

A jury too frequently have at least one member more ready to hang the panel than to hang the traitor.

> Letter to Erastus Corning and Others, [June 12] 1863, reprinted in *Collected Works of Abraham Lincoln*, v. 6, p. 264. Rutgers University Press (1953, 1990).

JUSTICE

The severest justice may not always be the best policy.

> "Address to the Senate and House of Representatives," July 17, 1862, reprinted in *Collected Works of Abraham Lincoln*, v. 5, p. 330. Rutgers University Press (1953, 1990).

KNOWLEDGE

If a man says he *knows* a thing, then he must show *how* he knows it.

> "First Debate with Stephen A. Douglas at Ottawa, Illinois," August 21, 1858, reprinted in *Collected Works of Abraham Lincoln*, v. 3, p. 14. Rutgers University Press (1953, 1990).

LABOR

In the early days of the world, the Almighty said to the first of our race "In the sweat of thy face shalt thou eat bread"; and since then, if we except the *light* and the *air* of heaven, no good thing has been, or can be enjoyed by us, without having first cost labor.

> "Fragments of a Tariff Discussion," [December 1, 1847?], reprinted in *Collected Works of Abraham Lincoln*, v. 1, p. 411. Rutgers University Press (1953, 1990).

It has so happened in all ages of the world, that *some* have labored, and *others* have, without labor, enjoyed a large proportion of the fruits.

> "Fragments of a Tariff Discussion," [December 1, 1847?], reprinted in *Collected Works of Abraham Lincoln*, v. 1, p. 412. Rutgers University Press (1953, 1990).

As Labor is the common *burthen* of our race, so the effort of *some* to shift their share of the burthen on to the shoulders of *others*, is the great, durable, curse of the race.

> "Fragment on Free Labor," [September 17, 1859?], reprinted in *Collected Works of Abraham Lincoln*, v. 3, p. 462. Rutgers University Press (1953, 1990).

To [secure] to each laborer the whole product of his labor, or as nearly as possible, is a most worthy object of any good government.

"Fragments of a Tariff Discussion," [December 1, 1847?], reprinted in *Collected Works of Abraham Lincoln*, v. 1, p. 412. Rutgers University Press (1953, 1990).

And, inasmuch [as] most good things are produced by labor, it follows that [all] such things of right belong to those whose labor has produced them.

"Fragments of a Tariff Discussion," [December 1, 1847?], reprinted in *Collected Works of Abraham Lincoln*, v. 1, p. 412. Rutgers University Press (1953, 1990).

Free labor has the inspiration of hope; pure slavery has no hope.

"Fragment on Free Labor," [September 17, 1859?], reprinted in *Collected Works of Abraham Lincoln*, v. 3, p. 462. Rutgers University Press (1953, 1990).

Labor is prior to, and independent of, capital. Capital is only the fruit of labor, and could never have existed if labor had not first existed. Labor is the superior of capital, and deserves much the higher consideration.

"Annual Message to Congress," December 3, 1861, reprinted in *Collected Works of Abraham Lincoln*, v. 5, p.52. Rutgers University Press (1953, 1990).

It is assumed that whoever is once a hired laborer, is fixed in that condition for life. Now, there is no such relation between capital and labor as assumed; nor is there any such thing as a free man being fixed for life in the condition of a hired laborer.

"Annual Message to Congress," December 3, 1861, reprinted in *Collected Works of Abraham Lincoln*, v. 5, p. 52. Rutgers University Press (1953, 1990).

Labor is the true standard of value.

"Speech at Pittsburgh, Pennsylvania," February 15, 1861, reprinted in *Collected Works of Abraham Lincoln*, v. 4, p. 212. Rutgers University Press (1953, 1990).

Labor is like any other commodity in the market—increase the demand for it, and you increase the price of it.

"Annual Message to Congress," December 1, 1862, reprinted in *Collected Works of Abraham Lincoln*, v. 5, p. 535. Rutgers University Press (1953, 1990).

The strongest bond of human sympathy, outside of the family relation, should be one uniting all working people, of all nations, and tongues, and kindreds.

"Reply to the New York Workingmen's Democratic Republican Association," March 21, 1864, reprinted in *Collected Works of Abraham Lincoln*, v. 7, p. 259. Rutgers University Press (1953, 1990).

The existing rebellion ... is, in fact, a war upon the rights of all working people.

"Reply to New York Workingmen's Democratic Republican Association," March 21, 1864, reprinted in *Collected Works of Abraham Lincoln*, v. 7, p. 259. Rutgers University Press (1953, 1990).

LAW

Let every American, every lover of liberty, every well wisher to his posterity, swear by the blood of the Revolution, never to violate in the least particular, the laws of the country; and never to tolerate their violation by others.

"Lyceum Address," Springfield, Illinois, January 27, 1838, reprinted in *Collected Works of Abraham Lincoln*, v. 1, p. 112. Rutgers University Press (1953, 1990).

Let reverence for the laws be breathed by every American mother to the lisping babe that prattles on her lap; let it be taught in schools, in seminaries, and in colleges; let it be written in Primers, spelling books, and in Almanacs; let it be preached from the pulpit, proclaimed in legislative halls, and enforced in courts of justice. And, in short, let it become the *political religion* of the nation; and let the old and the young, the rich and the poor, the grave and the gay, of all sexes and tongues, and colors and conditions, sacrifice unceasingly upon its altars.

"Lyceum Address," Springfield, Illinois, January 27, 1838, reprinted in *Collected Works of Abraham Lincoln, Supplement 1832-1865*, v. 1, p. 108. Rutgers University Press (1974).

Let me not be understood as saying there are no bad laws, nor that grievances may not arise, for the redress of which, no legal provisions have been made. I mean to say no such thing. But I do mean to say, that, although bad laws, if they exist, should be repealed as soon as possible, still while they continue in force, for the sake of example, they should be religiously observed.

"Lyceum Address," Springfield, Illinois, January 27, 1838, reprinted in *Collected Works of Abraham Lincoln*, v. 1, p. 112. Rutgers University Press (1953, 1990).

He who asks equity must do equity.

"Pencilled Notes," n.d., reprinted in *Collected Works of Abraham Lincoln, Supplement 1832-1865*, v. 10, p. 288. Rutgers University Press (1974).

That *is* good book-law; but is not the rule of actual practice.

"Speech at Peoria, Illinois," October 16, 1854, reprinted in *Collected Works of Abraham Lincoln*, v. 2, p. 262. Rutgers University Press (1953, 1990).

Legislation and *adjudication* must follow, and conform to, the progress
of society.

> "Notes of argument in a law case," [June 1858?], reprinted in *Collected Works of Abraham Lincoln*, v. 2,
> p. 459. Rutgers University Press (1953, 1990).

A law may be both constitutional and expedient, and yet may be
administered in an unjust and unfair way.

> "Opinion on the Draft," [September 14?], 1863, reprinted in *Collected Works of Abraham Lincoln*, v. 6,
> p. 448. Rutgers University Press (1953, 1990).

I think the Constitution invests its commander-in-chief with the law of
war in time of war.

> Letter to James C. Conkling, August 26, 1843, reprinted in *Collected Works of Abraham Lincoln*, v. 6,
> p. 408. Rutgers University Press (1953, 1990).

*L*AWYERS

My way of living leads me to be about the courts of justice; and there, I
have sometimes seen a good lawyer, struggling for his client's neck, in a
desperate case, employing every artifice to work round, befog, and cover
up, with many words, some point arising in the case, which he *dared* not
admit, and yet *could* not deny.

> Speech in United States House of Representatives: "The War with Mexico," January 12, 1848, reprinted
> in *Collected Works of Abraham Lincoln*, v. 1, p. 438. Rutgers University Press (1953, 1990).

In law it is good policy to never *plead* what you *need* not, lest you oblige
yourself to *prove* what you *can* not.

> Letter to Usher F. Linder, February 20, 1848, reprinted in *Collected Works of Abraham Lincoln*, v. 1,
> p. 453. Rutgers University Press (1953, 1990).

The leading rule for the lawyer, as for the man of every other calling
is *diligence*. Leave nothing for to-morrow which can be done to-day.
Never let your correspondence fall behind. Whatever piece of business
you have in hand, before stopping, do all the labor pertaining to it
which can *then* be done.

> Fragment: "Notes for a Law Lecture," [July 1, 1850?], reprinted in *Collected Works of Abraham
> Lincoln*, v. 10, p. 18. Rutgers University Press (1953, 1990).

Extemporaneous speaking should be practiced and cultivated. It is the
lawyer's avenue to the public. However able and faithful he may be in other

respects, people are slow to bring him business if he cannot make a speech. And yet there is not a more fatal error to young lawyers than relying too much on speech-making. If any one, upon his rare powers of speaking, shall claim an exemption from the drudgery of the law, his case is a failure in advance.

> Fragment: "Notes for a Law Lecture," [July 1, 1850?], reprinted in *Collected Works of Abraham Lincoln*, v. 2, p. 81. Rutgers University Press (1953, 1990).

Discourage litigation. Persuade your neighbors to compromise whenever you can. Point out to them how the nominal winner is often a real loser—in fees, expenses, and waste of time. As a peacemaker the lawyer has a superior opportunity of being a good man. There will still be business enough.

> Fragment: "Notes for a Law Lecture," [July 1, 1850?], reprinted in *Collected Works of Abraham Lincoln*, v. 2, p. 81. Rutgers University Press (1953, 1990).

Resolve to be honest at all events; and if in your own judgment you cannot be an honest lawyer, resolve to be honest without being a lawyer. Choose some other occupation, rather than one in the choosing of which you do, in advance, consent to be a knave.

> Fragment: "Notes for a Law Lecture," [July 1, 1850?], reprinted in *Collected Works of Abraham Lincoln*, v. 2, p. 82. Rutgers University Press (1953, 1990).

There is a vague popular belief that lawyers are necessarily dishonest. I say vague, because when we consider to what extent confidence and honors are reposed in and conferred upon lawyers by the people, it appears improbable that their impression of dishonesty is very distinct and vivid. Yet the impression is common, almost universal.

> Fragment: "Notes for a Law Lecture," [July 1, 1850?], reprinted in *Collected Works of Abraham Lincoln*, v. 2, p. 82. Rutgers University Press (1953, 1990).

I understand that it is a maxim of law, that a poor plea may be a good plea to a bad declaration.

> "Third Debate with Stephen A. Douglas at Jonesboro, Illinois," September 15, 1858, reprinted in *Collected Works of Abraham Lincoln*, v. 3, p. 123. Rutgers University Press (1953, 1990).

*L*EADERSHIP

Such a man the times have demanded, and such, in the providence of God was given us. But he is gone. Let us strive . . . that, in future national emergencies, He will not fail to provide us the instruments of safety and security.

"Eulogy on Henry Clay," July 6, 1852, reprinted in *Collected Works of Abraham Lincoln*, v. 2, p. 132. Rutgers University Press (1953, 1990).

LEGISLATION

But what are they to do? The whole are strung together; and they must take all, or reject all. They can not take what they like, and leave the rest. . . . They shut their eyes, and gulp the whole.

"Speech in the U.S. House of Representatives on the Presidential Question," July 27, 1848, reprinted in *Collected Works of Abraham Lincoln*, v. 1, p. 505. Rutgers University Press (1953, 1990).

LETTERS

You see by this, that I am neither dead nor quite crazy yet.

Letter to John T. Stuart, February 3, 1841, reprinted in *Collected Works of Abraham Lincoln, Supplement 1832-1865*, v. 10, p.06. Rutgers University Press (1953, 1990).

I am ashamed of not sooner answering your letter, herewith returned; and, my only apologies are, first, that I have been very busy in the U.S. court; and second, that when I received the letter I put it in my old hat, and buying a new one the next day, the old one was set aside, and so, the letter lost sight of for a time.

Letter to Richard S. Thomas, June 27, 1850, reprinted in *Collected Works of Abraham Lincoln*, v. 2, p. 80. Rutgers University Press (1953, 1990).

Yours of the 29th of June was duly received. I did not answer it, because it plagued me.

Letter to James W. Grimes, July 12, 1856, reprinted in *Collected Works of Abraham Lincoln*, v. 2, p. 348. Rutgers University Press (1953, 1990).

Don't make your letters so short as mine.

Letter to Elihu B. Washburne, May 26, 1860, reprinted in *Collected Works of Abraham Lincoln*, v. 4, p. 56. Rutgers University Press (1953, 1990).

*L*IES

He who makes an assertion without knowing whether it is true or false, is guilty of falsehood. . . .

> Letter to Allen N. Ford, August 11, 1846, reprinted in *Collected Works of Abraham Lincoln*, v. 1, p. 384. Rutgers University Press (1953, 1990).
>
> See also TRUTH

This open attempt to prove, by telling the *truth*, what he could not prove by telling the *whole truth*. . . .

> Speech in the United States House of Representatives: "The War with Mexico," January 12, 1848, reprinted in *Collected Works of Abraham Lincoln*, v. 1, p. 432. Rutgers University Press (1953, 1990).
>
> President Polk's explanation for the coming of the War with Mexico.

A specious and fantastic arrangement of words, by which a man can prove a horse chestnut to be a chestnut horse.

> "First Debate with Stephen A. Douglas at Ottawa, Illinois," August 21, 1858, reprinted in *Collected Works of Abraham Lincoln*, v. 3, p. 16. Rutgers University Press (1953, 1990).

This he cannot deny; and so he remembers to forget it.

> Fragment: "Notes for Speeches," [c. August 21, 1858], reprinted in *Collected Works of Abraham Lincoln*, v. 2, p. 552. Rutgers University Press (1953, 1990).
>
> Stephen Douglas' early views on banking.

I say that you took your hat off your head, and you prove me a liar by putting it on your head.

> "Fourth Debate with Stephen A. Douglas at Charleston, Illinois," September 18, 1858, reprinted in *Collected Works of Abraham Lincoln*, v. 3, p. 185. Rutgers University Press (1953, 1990).

You can fool all the people some of the time and some of the people all the time, but you cannot fool all the people all the time.

> "Speech at Clinton, Illinois," September 8, 1858, reprinted in *Complete Works of Abraham Lincoln*, v. 3, p. 349. Tandy (1905).
>
> Though from a quite questionable source, the statement is Lincolnesque and is indelibly tied to him.

*L*OOKS

I have stepped out upon this platform that I may see you and that you may see me, and in the arrangement I have the best of the bargain.

> "Remarks at Pinesville, Ohio," February 16, 1861, reprinted in *Collected Works of Abraham Lincoln*, v. 4, p. 218. Rutgers University Press (1953, 1990).
>
> See also PEOPLE (last quotation)

*L*OVE *LETTERS*

The longer I can avoid the mortification of looking in the Post Office for your letter and not finding it, the better. You see I am mad about that *old letter* yet.

Letter to Mary S. Owens, December 13, 1836, reprinted in *Collected Works of Abraham Lincoln*, v. 1, p. 54. Rutgers University Press (1953, 1990).

*M*AJORITY *AND* MINORITY

They are the majority, and therefore have both the legal and moral right to have their interest first consulted.

"Fragments of a Tariff Discussion," [December 1, 1847?], reprinted in *Collected Works of Abraham Lincoln*, v. 1, p. 414. Rutgers University Press (1953, 1990).

The majority may not choose to remain permanently rebuked by that [any] minority.

"Speech at a Republican Banquet, Chicago, Illinois," December 10, 1856, reprinted in *Collected Works of Abraham Lincoln*, v. 2, p. 384. Rutgers University Press (1953, 1990).

If, by the mere force of numbers, a majority should deprive a minority of any clearly written constitutional right, it might, in a moral point of view, justify revolution—certainly would, if such right were a vital one.

"First Inaugural Address," March 4, 1861, reprinted in *Collected Works of Abraham Lincoln*, v. 4, p. 262. Rutgers University Press (1953, 1990).

If the majority does not control, the minority must—would that be right? . . . Though the majority may be wrong, and I will not undertake to say that they were not wrong in electing me, yet we must adhere to the principle that the majority shall rule.

"Speech at Steubenville," Ohio, February 14, 1861, reprinted in *Collected Works of Abraham Lincoln*, v. 4, p. 207. Rutgers University Press (1953, 1990).

A majority, held in restraint by constitutional checks and limitations, and always changing easily with deliberate changes of popular opinions and sentiments, is the only true sovereign of a free people.

"First Inaugural Address," March 4, 1861, reprinted in *Collected Works of Abraham Lincoln*, v. 4, p. 268. Rutgers University Press (1953, 1990).

If the minority will not acquiesce, the majority must or the government must cease.

"First Inaugural Address," March 4, 1861, reprinted in *Collected Works of Abraham Lincoln*, v. 4, p. 268. Rutgers University Press (1953, 1990).

The rule of a minority as a permanent arrangement is wholly inadmissable.

"First Inaugural Address," March 4, 1861, reprinted in *Collected Works of Abraham Lincoln*, v. 4, p. 268. Rutgers University Press (1953, 1990).

$\mathcal{M}$ALICE

I shall do nothing in malice. What I deal with is too vast for malicious dealing.

Letter to Cuthbert Bullitt, July 28, 1862, reprinted in *Collected Works of Abraham Lincoln*, v. 5, p. 346. Rutgers University Press (1953, 1990).

So long as I have been here I have not willingly planted a thorn in any man's bosom.

"Response to a Serenade," November 10, 1864, reprinted in *Collected Works of Abraham Lincoln*, v. 8, p. 101. Rutgers University Press (1953, 1990).

With malice toward none; with charity for all. . . .

"Second Inaugural Address," March 4, 1865, reprinted in *Collected Works of Abraham Lincoln*, v. 8, p. 333. Rutgers University Press (1953, 1990).

$\mathcal{M}$ARCHING

Our men are not moles, and can't dig under the earth; they are not birds, and can't fly through the air. There is no way but to march across, and that they must do.

"Reply to the Baltimore Committee," April 22, 1861, reprinted in *Collected Works of Abraham Lincoln*, v. 4, p. 342. Rutgers University Press (1953, 1990).

$\mathcal{M}$ARRIAGE

I have now come to the conclusion never again to think of marrying; and for this reason; I can never be satisfied with any one who would be block-head enough to have me.

Letter to Mrs. Orville H. Browning, April 1, 1838, reprinted in *Collected Works of Abraham Lincoln*, v. 1, p. 119. Rutgers University Press (1953, 1990).

But you say you *reasoned* yourself *into* it. What do you mean by that? Was it not that you found yourself unable to *reason* yourself *out of it*?

Letter to Joshua F. Speed, [January 3, 1842?], reprinted in *Collected Works of Abraham Lincoln*, v. 1, p. 266. Rutgers University Press (1953, 1990).

My old Father used to have a saying that "If you make a bad bargain, *hug* it the tighter;" and it occurs to me, that if the bargain you have just closed can possibly be called a bad one, it is certainly the most *pleasant one* for applying that maxim to, which my fancy can, by any effort, picture.

Letter to Joshua F. Speed, February 25, 1842, reprinted in *Collected Works of Abraham Lincoln*, v. 1, p. 280. Rutgers University Press (1953, 1990).

Nothing new here, except my marrying, which to me is a matter of profound wonder.

Letter to Samuel D. Marshall, November 11, 1842, reprinted in *Collected Works of Abraham Lincoln*, v. 1, p. 304. Rutgers University Press (1953, 1990).

In this troublesome world, we are never quite satisfied. When you were here, I thought you hindered me some in attending to business; but now, having nothing but business—no variety—it has grown exceedingly tasteless to me. I hate to sit down and direct documents, and I hate to stay in this old room by myself.

Letter to Mary Todd Lincoln, April 16, 1848, reprinted in *Collected Works of Abraham Lincoln*, v. 1, p. 465. Rutgers University Press (1953, 1990).

Come on just as soon as you can. I want to see you, and our dear-*dear* boys very much. . . .

Letter to Mary Todd Lincoln, June 12, 1848, reprinted in *Collected Works of Abraham Lincoln*, v. 1, p. 478. Rutgers University Press (1953, 1990).

He had concluded to give them "the long and the short of it!"

"Remarks at Leaman Place, Pennsylvania," February 22, 1861, reprinted in *Collected Works of Abraham Lincoln*, v. 4, p. 242. Rutgers University Press (1953, 1990).

On introducing himself (6′4″) and wife Mary Todd (5′3″).

*M*AXIM *FOR ALL SEASONS*

It is said an Eastern monarch once charged his wise men to invent him a sentence, to be ever in view, and which should be true and appropriate in all times and situations. They presented him the words: *"And this, too, shall pass away."*

"Address before the Wisconsin State Agricultural Society, Milwaukee, Wisconsin," September 30, 1859, reprinted in *Collected Works of Abraham Lincoln*, v. 3, p. 481. Rutgers University Press (1953, 1990).

*M*C*CLELLAN, GENERAL GEORGE B.*

It is indispensable to *you* that you strike a blow. . . . I beg to assure you that I have never written you, or spoken to you, in greater kindness of feeling than now, nor with a fuller purpose to sustain you, so far as in my most anxious judgment, I consistently can. *But you must act.*

> Letter to General George B. McClellan, April 9, 1862, reprinted in *Collected Works of Abraham Lincoln*, v. 5, p. 185. Rutgers University Press (1953, 1990).

Your call for Parrott guns from Washington alarms me—chiefly because it argues indefinite procrastination. Is anything to be done?

> Letter to General George B. McClellan, May 1, 1862, reprinted in *Collected Works of Abraham Lincoln*, v. 5, p. 203. Rutgers University Press (1953, 1990).

You are probably engaged with the enemy. I suppose he made the attack.

> Letter to General George B. McClellan, June 1, 1862, reprinted in *Collected Works of Abraham Lincoln*, v. 5, p. 255. Rutgers University Press (1953, 1990).

Stand well on your guard—hold all your ground, or yield any only, inch by inch and in good order.

> Letter to General George B. McClellan, June 1, 1862, reprinted in *Collected Works of Abraham Lincoln*, v. 5, p. 255. Rutgers University Press (1953, 1990).

He is a brave and able man.

> "Address to Union Meeting of Washington," August 6, 1862, reprinted in *Collected Works of Abraham Lincoln*, v. 5, p. 358. Rutgers University Press (1953, 1990).

Are you not over-cautious when you assume that you can not do what the enemy is constantly doing? Should you not claim to be at least his equal in prowess and act upon the claim?

> Letter to General George B. McClellan, October 13, 1862, reprinted in *Collected Works of Abraham Lincoln*, v. 5, p. 460. Rutgers University Press (1953, 1990).

General McClellan and myself are to be photographed . . . if we can be still long enough. I feel General McClellan should have no problem. . . .

> Letter to Mary Todd Lincoln, October, 1862, *manuscript*, courtesy of Lloyd Ostendorff.

I have just read your dispatch about sore tongued and fatigued horses. Will you pardon me for asking what the horses of your army have done since the battle of Antietem that fatigue anything?

> Letter to General George B. McClellan, October 24, 1862, reprinted in *Collected Works of Abraham Lincoln*, v. 5, p. 474. Rutgers University Press (1953, 1990).

$\mathcal{M}$EADE, GENERAL GEORGE G.

Do not lean a hair's breadth against your own feelings, or your judgment of the public service, on the idea of gratifying me.

Letter to General George G. Meade, July 27, 1863, reprinted in *Collected Works of Abraham Lincoln*, v. 6, p. 350. Rutgers University Press (1953, 1990).

If General Meade can now attack him [General Robert E. Lee] on a field no worse than equal for us, and will do so with all the skill and courage, which he, his officers and men possess, the honor will be his if he succeeds, and the blame may be mine if he fails.

Letter to General Henry W. Halleck, October 16, 1863, reprinted in *Collected Works of Abraham Lincoln*, v. 6, p. 518. Rutgers University Press (1953, 1990).

See also GETTYSBURG

$\mathcal{M}$ELANCHOLY

There is but one thing about her, so far as I could perceive, that I would have otherwise than as it is. That is something of a tendency to melancholy. This, let it be observed, is a misfortune not a fault.

Letter to Mary Speed, September 27, 1841, reprinted in *Collected Works of Abraham Lincoln*, v. 1, p. 261. Rutgers University Press (1953, 1990).

$\mathcal{M}$EMORY

As leaving some grand waterfall,
    We, lingering, list its roar—
So memory will hallow all
    We've known, but know no more.

"My Childhood Home I See Again," [c. September 18, 1846,] reprinted in *Collected Works of Abraham Lincoln*, v. 1, p. 379. Rutgers University Press (1953, 1990).

The world will little note, nor long remember what we say here, but it can never forget what they did here.

"Gettysburg Address," Final Draft, November 19, 1863, reprinted in *Collected Works of Abraham Lincoln*, v. 7, p. 23. Rutgers University Press (1953, 1990).

$\mathcal{M}$EN

Man is a land animal. . . .

"First Lecture on Discoveries and Inventions," [April 6, 1858], reprinted in *Collected Works of Abraham Lincoln*, v. 2, p. 440. Rutgers University Press (1953, 1990).

Gold is good in its place; but living, brave, patriotic men, are better than gold.

"Response to a Serenade," November 10, 1864, reprinted in *Collected Works of Abraham Lincoln*, v. 8, p. 101. Rutgers University Press (1953, 1990).

The most important branch of national resources—that of living men.

"Annual Message to Congress," December 6, 1864, reprinted in *Collected Works of Abraham Lincoln*, v. 8, p. 150. Rutgers University Press (1953, 1990).

$\mathcal{M}$EN AND MEASURES

It was not the election of General [William Henry] Harrison that was expected to produce happy effects, but the measures to be adopted by his administration.

"Campaign Circular from Whig Committee," March 4, 1843, reprinted in *Collected Works of Abraham Lincoln*, v. 1, p. 317. Rutgers University Press (1953, 1990).

$\mathcal{M}$ILITARY ADVICE

Can you get near enough to throw shells into the city?

Letter to General George B. McClellan, May 26, 1862, reprinted in *Collected Works of Abraham Lincoln*, v. 5, p. 240. Rutgers University Press (1953, 1990).

Neither you, nor Napoleon, if he were alive again, could get any good out of an army, while such a spirit [of division] prevails in it.

Letter to General Joseph Hooker, Jan 26, 1863, reprinted in *Collected Works of Abraham Lincoln*, v. 6, p. 79. Rutgers University Press (1953, 1990).

$\mathcal{M}$ILITARY COMMANDERS

If the military commanders in the field cannot be successful, not only the

Secretary of War, but myself for the time being the master of them both, cannot be but failures.

"Address to Union Meeting at Washington," April 6, 1862, reprinted in *Collected Works of Abraham Lincoln*, v. 5, p. 359. Rutgers University Press (1953, 1990).

*M*ILITARY GLORY

The exceeding brightness of military glory—that attractive rainbow, that rises in showers of blood—that serpent's eye, that charms to destroy. . . .

"Speech in United States House of Representatives on the War with Mexico," January 12, 1848, reprinted in *Collected Works of Abraham Lincoln*, v. 1, p. 439. Rutgers University Press (1953, 1990).

*M*ILITARY PROMOTION

Seniority has not been my rule, in this connection; but in considering military merit, it seems to me the world has abundant evidence that I discard politics.

Letter to William R. Morrison, November 5, 1862, reprinted in *Collected Works of Abraham Lincoln*, v. 5, p. 486. Rutgers University Press (1953, 1990).

*M*ILITARY RANK

Truth to speak, I do not appreciate this matter of rank on paper, as you officers do. The world will not forget that you fought the battle of "Stone River" and it will never care a fig whether you rank General Grant on paper, or he so ranks you.

Letter to General William S. Rosecrans, March 17, 1863, reprinted in *Collected Works of Abraham Lincoln*, v. 6, p. 139. Rutgers University Press (1953, 1990).

*M*ILITARY ROLE

You do not mix politics with your profession, in which you are right.

Letter to General Joseph Hooker, January 26, 1863, reprinted in *Collected Works of Abraham Lincoln*, v. 6, p. 78. Rutgers University Press (1953, 1990).

The President directs me to say to you that he wishes you to have no conference with General Lee unless it be for the capitulation of General Lee's army, or on some minor, and purely, military matter. He instructs me to say that you are not to decide, discuss, or confer upon any political question. Such questions the President holds in his own hands; and will submit them to no military conferences or conventions. Meantime you are to press to the utmost your military advantages.

> Letter to General Ulysses S. Grant, March 3, 1865, reprinted in *Collected Works of Abraham Lincoln*, v. 8, p. 330. Rutgers University Press (1953, 1990).

*M*ILITARY STRATEGY

I state my general idea of this war to be that we have the *greater* numbers, and the enemy has the *greater* facility of concentrating forces upon points of collision; that we must fail, unless we can find some way of making *our* advantage an over-match for *his;* and that this can only be done by menacing him with superior forces at *different* points, at the *same* time; so that we can safely attack, one, or both, if he makes no change; and if he *weakens* one to *strengthen* the other, forbear to attack the strengthened one, but seize, and hold the weakened one, gaining so much.

> Letter to General Don C. Buell, January 13, 1862, reprinted in *Collected Works of Abraham Lincoln*, v. 5, p. 98. Rutgers University Press (1953, 1990).

If we can not beat him when he bears the wastage of coming to us [in the North], we never can when we bear the wastage of going to him. This proposition is a simple truth, and is too important to be lost sight of for a moment. In coming to us, he tenders us an advantage which we should not waive. We should not so operate as to merely drive him away. As we must beat him somewhere, or fail finally. . . .

> Letter to General George B. McClellan, October 13, 1862, reprinted in *Collected Works of Abraham Lincoln*, v. 5, p. 461. Rutgers University Press (1953, 1990).

The army, like the nation, has become demoralized by the idea that the war is to be ended, the nation united, and peace restored, by *strategy*, and not by hard desperate fighting.

> "Memorandum on Furloughs," November, 1862, reprinted in *Collected Works of Abraham Lincoln*, v. 5, p. 484. Rutgers University Press (1953, 1990).

This expanding, and piling up of *impedimenta*, has been, so far, almost our ruin, and will be our final ruin if it is not abandoned.

> Letter to Nathaniel P. Banks, November 22, 1862, reprinted in *Collected Works of Abraham Lincoln*, v. 5, p. 505. Rutgers University Press (1953, 1990).

Our prime object is the enemies' army in front of us, and is not with, or about, Richmond—at all, unless it be incidental to the main object.

> "Memorandum on Joseph Hooker's Plan of Campaign Against Richmond," [c. April 6-10, 1863], reprinted in *Collected Works of Abraham Lincoln*, v. 6, p. 164. Rutgers University Press (1953, 1990).

I would not take any risk of being entangled upon the river, like an ox jumped half over a fence, and liable to be torn by dogs, front and rear, without a fair chance to gore one way or kick the other.

> Letter to General Joseph Hooker, June 5, 1863, reprinted in *Collected Works of Abraham Lincoln*, v. 6, p. 249. Rutgers University Press (1953, 1990).

For a battle, then, General Meade has three men to General Lee's two. Yet, it having been determined that choosing ground, and standing on the defensive, gives so great advantage that the three can not safely attack the two, the three are left simply standing on the defensive also. If the enemy's sixty thousand are sufficient to keep our ninety thousand away from Richmond, why, by the same rule, may not forty thousand of ours keep their sixty thousand away from Washington, leaving us fifty thousand to put to some other use? . . . Unless we admit we are not the equal of the enemy man for man.

> Letter to General Henry W. Halleck, September 19, 1863, reprinted in *Collected Works of Abraham Lincoln*, v. 6, p. 467. Rutgers University Press (1953, 1990).

I have constantly desired the Army of the Potomac to make Lee's army, and not Richmond, its objective point.

> Letter to General Henry W. Halleck, September 19, 1863, reprinted in *Collected Works of Abraham Lincoln*, v. 6, p. 467. Rutgers University Press (1953, 1990).

I have seen your dispatch in which you say "I want Sheridan put in command of all the troops in the field, with instructions to put himself South of the enemy, and follow him to the death. Wherever the enemy goes, let our troops go also." This, I think, is exactly right, as to how our forces should move. But. . . it will neither be done nor attempted unless you watch it every day, and hour, and force it.

> Letter to General Ulysses S. Grant, August 3, 1864, reprinted in *Collected Works of Abraham Lincoln*, v. 7, p. 476. Rutgers University Press (1953, 1990).

I have seen your dispatch expressing your unwillingness to break your hold where you are. Neither am I willing. Hold on with a bull-dog grip, and chew and choke, as much as possible.

> Letter to General Ulysses S. Grant, August 17, 1864, reprinted in *Collected Works of Abraham Lincoln*, v. 7, p. 499. Rutgers University Press (1953, 1990).

General Sheridan says "If the thing is pressed I think that Lee will surrender." Let the *thing* be pressed.

> Letter to General Ulysses S. Grant, April 7, 1865, reprinted in *Collected Works of Abraham Lincoln*, v. 8, p. 392. Rutgers University Press (1953, 1990).

MINISTERS AND LAWYERS

Preachers, lawyers, and hired agents. Between these and the mass of mankind, there is a want of *approachability*. . . .

> "Temperance Address," February 22, 1842, reprinted in *Collected Works of Abraham Lincoln*, v. 1, p. 272. Rutgers University Press (1953, 1990).

MISREPRESENTATION

When a man hears himself somewhat misrepresented, it provokes him—at least, I find it so with myself; but when the misrepresentation becomes very gross and palpable, it is more apt to amuse him.

> "First Debate with Stephen A. Douglas at Ottawa, Illinois," August 21, 1858, reprinted in *Collected Works of Abraham Lincoln*, v. 3, p. 13. Rutgers University Press (1953, 1990).

I have found that it is not entirely safe, when one is misrepresented under his very nose, to allow the misrepresentation to go uncontradicted.

> "Speech at Columbus, Ohio," September 16, 1859, reprinted in *Collected Works of Abraham Lincoln*, v. 3, p. 401. Rutgers University Press (1953, 1990).

MISSISSIPPI RIVER

The signs look better. The Father of Waters again goes unvexed to the sea.

> Letter to James C. Conkling, August 26, 1863, reprinted in *Collected Works of Abraham Lincoln*, v. 6, p. 409. Rutgers University Press (1953, 1990).

*M*OBS

Having ever regarded Government as their deadliest bane, they make a jubilee of the suspension of its operations; and pray for nothing so much, as its total annihilation.

"Lyceum Address," Springfield, Illinois, January 27, 1838, reprinted in *Collected Works of Abraham Lincoln*, v. 1, p. 111. Rutgers University Press (1953, 1990).

There is no grievance that is a fit object of redress by mob law.

"Lyceum Address," Springfield, Illinois, January 27, 1838, reprinted in *Collected Works of Abraham Lincoln*, v. 1, p. 113. Rutgers University Press (1953, 1990).

Whenever the vicious portion of population shall be permitted to gather in bands . . . and burn churches, ravage and rob provision stores, throw printing presses into rivers, shoot editors, and hang and burn obnoxious persons at pleasure, and with impunity; depend on it, this Government cannot last.

"Lyceum Address," Springfield, Illinois, January 27, 1838, reprinted in *Collected Works of Abraham Lincoln*, v. 1, p. 111. Rutgers University Press (1953, 1990).

Judge Lynch sometimes take jurisdiction of cases which prove too strong for the courts; but this is the first case within my knowledge, wherein the court being able to maintain jurisdiction against Judge Lynch, the military has come to assistance of the latter.

Letter to General James G. Blunt, August 18, 1863, reprinted in *Collected Works of Abraham Lincoln*, v. 6, p. 396. Rutgers University Press (1953, 1990).

General Blunt reported that "murderers and thieves" had been hanged by "honest people" in Kansas.

*M*ONETARY POLICY

Who can contemplate, without terror, the distress, ruin, bankruptcy and beggary, that must follow [mistaken governmental policies].

"Speech on the Sub-Treasury," December 26, 1839, reprinted in *Collected Works of Abraham Lincoln*, v. 1, p. 162. Rutgers University Press (1953, 1990).

*M*ONEY

Money is only valuable while in circulation. . . .

"Speech on the Sub-Treasury," December 26, 1839, reprinted in *Collected Works of Abraham Lincoln*, v. 1, p. 160. Rutgers University Press (1953, 1990).

We do not pretend that a National Bank can establish and maintain a sound and uniform state of currency in the country, in *spite* of the National Government; but we do say that it has established and maintained such a currency, and can so do again, by the *aid* of that Government; and we further say that no duty is more imperative on that Government, than the duty it owes the people, of furnishing them a sound and uniform currency.

"Speech on the Sub-Treasury," December 26, 1839, reprinted in *Collected Works of Abraham Lincoln*, v. 1, p. 164. Rutgers University Press (1953, 1990).

It is an old maxim and a very sound one that he that dances should always pay the fiddler. . . . I am decidedly opposed to the people's money being used to pay the fiddler.

"Speech in the Illinois Legislature Concerning the State Bank," January 11, 1837, reprinted in *Collected Works of Abraham Lincoln*, v. 1, p. 64. Rutgers University Press (1953, 1990).

Protect labor against the evils of a vicious currency, and facilitate commerce by cheap and safe exchanges.

"Annual Message to Congress," December 1, 1862, reprinted in *Collected Works of Abraham Lincoln*, v. 5, p. 523. Rutgers University Press (1953, 1990).

There is powerful temptation in money. . . .

Letter to William S. Rosecrans, March 17, 1863, reprinted in *Collected Works of Abraham Lincoln*, v. 6, p. 138. Rutgers University Press (1953, 1990).

The plainest print cannot be read through a gold eagle.

"Speech at Springfield, Illinois," June 26, 1857, reprinted in *Collected Works of Abraham Lincoln*, v. 2, p. 409. Rutgers University Press (1953, 1990).

*M*ORALITY

They must blow out the moral lights around us; they must penetrate the human soul, and eradicate there the love of liberty; and then, and not till then, could they perpetuate slavery in this country.

"Speech at Bloomington, Illinois," September 4, 1858, reprinted in *Collected Works of Abraham Lincoln*, v. 3, p. 89. Rutgers University Press (1953, 1990).

See also SLAVERY

$\mathcal{M}$OTIVATION

Why build the cage if they expect to catch no birds?

"Speech on the Sub-Treasury," December 26, 1839, reprinted in *Collected Works of Abraham Lincoln*, v. 1, p. 169. Rutgers University Press (1953, 1990).

$\mathcal{M}$URDER

Examinations were made of cellars, wells, and pits of all descriptions, where it was thought possible the body might be concealed. All the fresh, or tolerably fresh graves at the graveyard were pried into, and dead horses and dead dogs were disinterred, where, in some instances, they had been buried by their partial masters.

"The Trailor Murder Case," April 15, 1846, reprinted in *Collected Works of Abraham Lincoln*, v. 1, p. 373. Rutgers University Press (1953, 1990).

On the search for a supposed victim.

If I should be indicted for murder, and upon the trial it should be discovered that I had been implicated in that murder, but that the prosecuting witness was guilty too, that would not at all touch the question of my crime. It would be no relief to my neck that they discovered this other man who charged the crime upon me to be guilty too.

"Fourth Debate with Stephen A. Douglas at Charleston, Illinois," September 18, 1858, reprinted in *Collected Works of Abraham Lincoln*, v. 3, p. 151. Rutgers University Press (1953, 1990).

$\mathcal{N}$ATIONALISM

I . . . wish to be no less than National in all the positions I may take. . . .

"Speech at Peoria, Illinois," October 16, 1854, reprinted in *Collected Works of Abraham Lincoln*, v. 2, p. 248. Rutgers University Press (1953, 1990).

The national resources, then, are unexhausted and, as we believe, inexhaustible. The public purpose to re-establish and maintain the national authority is unchanged and, as we believe, unchangeable.

"Annual Message to Congress," December 6, 1864, reprinted in *Collected Works of Abraham Lincoln*, v. 8, p. 151. Rutgers University Press (1953, 1990).

NAVY

Nor must Uncle Sam's web-feet be forgotten. At all the watery margins they have been present. Not only on the deep sea, the broad bay, and the rapid river, but also up the narrow, muddy bayou, and wherever their ground was a little damp, they have been, and made their tracks.

> Letter to James C. Conkling, August 26, 1863, reprinted in *Collected Works of Abraham Lincoln*, v. 6, p. 409. Rutgers University Press (1953, 1990).

NECESSARY EVIL

One side ignored the *necessity,* and magnified the evils of the system; while the other ignored the evils, and magnified the necessity; and each bitterly assailed the motives of the other.

> Letter to Charles D. Drake and Others, October 5, 1863, reprinted in *Collected Works of Abraham Lincoln*, v. 6, p. 502. Rutgers University Press (1953, 1990).
>
> On politics in Missouri.

NEUTRALITY

A class of men who, having no choice of sides in the contest, were anxious only to have quiet and comfort for themselves while it rages, and to fall in with the victorious side at the end of it, without loss to themselves.... They are to touch neither a sail nor a pump, but to be merely passengers—dead-heads at that—to be carried snug and dry, through-out the storm, and safely landed right side up. Nay, more; even a mutineer is to go untouched lest these sacred passengers receive an accidental wound.

> Letter to Cuthbert Bullitt, July 28, 1862, reprinted in *Collected Works of Abraham Lincoln*, v. 5, p. 345. Rutgers University Press (1953, 1990).

NEW ENGLAND

Up here in New England, you have a soil that scarcely sprouts black-eyed beans, and yet where will you find wealthy men so wealthy, and poverty so rarely in extremity?

> "Speech at New Haven, Connecticut," March 6, 1860, reprinted in *Collected Works of Abraham Lincoln*, v. 4, p. 25. Rutgers University Press (1953, 1990).

NEWSPAPERS

The Secretary of War, you know, holds a pretty tight rein on the Press, so that they shall not tell more than they ought to, and I'm afraid that if I blab too much he might draw a tight rein on me.

"Remarks at Jersey City, New Jersey," June 24, 1862, reprinted in *Collected Works of Abraham Lincoln*, v. 5, p. 284. Rutgers University Press (1953, 1990).

NEWSPAPER REPORTERS: SOME OF THEM

Those villainous reporters. . . .

Letter To Martin P. Sweet, September 16, 1858, reprinted in *Collected Works of Abraham Lincoln*, v. 3, p. 144. Rutgers University Press (1953, 1990).

NIAGARA FALLS

It calls up the indefinite past. . . . The Mammoth and Mastadon—now so long dead that fragments of their monstrous bones alone testify that they ever lived, have gazed on Niagara. In that long, long time,never still for a single moment. Never dried, never froze, never slept, never rested. . . .

Fragment: "Niagara Falls," reprinted in *Collected Works of Abraham Lincoln*, v. 2, p. 10. Rutgers University Press (1953, 1990).

OBESITY

I knew she was over-size, but she now appeared a fair match for Falstaff. . . .

Letter to Mrs. Orville H. Browning, April 1, 1838, reprinted in *Collected Works of Abraham Lincoln*, v. 1, p. 118. Rutgers University Press (1953, 1990).

An unchivalrous comment after his marriage proposal was rejected.

OBSTINACY

Like some obstinate animal (I mean no disrespect,) that will hang on when he has once got his teeth fixed, you may cut off a leg, or you may tear away an arm, still he [Senator Douglas] will not relax his hold.

"First Debate with Stephen A. Douglas at Ottawa, Illinois," August 21, 1858, reprinted in *Collected Works of Abraham Lincoln*, v. 3, p. 28. Rutgers University Press (1953, 1990).

$\mathcal{P}_{AIN}$

I am sorry now to be the author of the slightest pain to you. But I was in such deep distress myself that I could not restrain some expression of it.

Letter to General George G. Meade, July 14, 1863, reprinted in *Collected Works of Abraham Lincoln*, v. 6, p. 327. Rutgers University Press (1953, 1990).

Referring to Lee's escape after Gettysburg.

As the proverb goes, no man knows so well where the shoe pinches as he who wears it.

Letter to Salmon P. Chase, June 28, 1864, reprinted in *Collected Works of Abraham Lincoln*, v. 7, p. 413. Rutgers University Press (1953, 1990).

$\mathcal{P}_{ARDONS}$

Would it not be wise to place a power of remission somewhere, so that these persons [rebels] may know they have something to lose by persisting, and something to save by desisting?

"To the Senate and House of Representatives," July 17, 1862, reprinted in *Collected Works of Abraham Lincoln*, v. 5, p. 330. Rutgers University Press (1953, 1990).

I knew him slightly. He was not of bad character at home, and I scarcely think he is guilty of any real crime. Please try if you cannot slip him through.

Letter to Joshua F. Speed, March 17, 1863, reprinted in *Collected Works of Abraham Lincoln*, v. 6, p. 140. Rutgers University Press (1953, 1990).

Referring to a man indicted in Kentucky for helping slave escape.

His own story is rather a bad one, and yet he tells it so frankly, that I am somewhat interested in him. Has he been a good soldier, except the desertion? About how old is he?

Letter to General George G. Meade, November 3, 1863, reprinted in *Collected Works of Abraham Lincoln*, v. 6, p. 561. Rutgers University Press (1953, 1990).

His story is unknown, though his life was saved by Lincoln.

The case of Andrews is really a very bad one, as appears by the record already before me. Yet before receiving this I had ordered his punishment commuted to imprisonment. . . . I did this, not on any merit in the case, but because I am trying to evade the butchering business lately.

"Endorsement Concerning Henry Andrews," January 7, 1864, reprinted in *Collected Works of Abraham Lincoln*, v. 7, p. 111. Rutgers University Press (1953, 1990).

Henry Andrews was tried for desertion.

Enlarge this man so long as he behaves himself.

> "Order Concerning William Patton," January 6, 1865, reprinted in *Collected Works of Abraham Lincoln, Supplement 1832-1865*, v. 10, p. 275. Rutgers University Press (1953, 1990).
>
> Former rebel, son of poor woman.

I can not say that the presumption in favor of their innocence has not been shaken; and yet it is very unsatisfactory to me that so many men of fair character should be convicted principally on the testimony of one single man and he of not quite fair character. It occurs to me that they have suffered enough, even if guilty, and enough for example I propose giving them a jubilee. . . .

> Letter to Joseph Holt, February 17, 1865, reprinted in *Collected Works of Abraham Lincoln*, v. 8, p. 303. Rutgers University Press (1953, 1990).
>
> Baltimore merchants who sent supplies to the Confederates.

The Doll Jack is pardoned by order of the President.

> "Pardon of Doll Jack," n.d., reprinted in *Collected Works of Abraham Lincoln*, v. 8, p. 425. Rutgers University Press (1953, 1990).
>
> Referring to his son's toy.

*P*ARENTS AND CHILDREN

If your Father and Mother desire you to come home, it is a delicate matter for me to advise you not to do it. Still, as you ask my advice, it is that if you are doing well, you better stick to it. . . . It can not be other than their first wish that you shall do well.

> Letter to John T. Hanks, September 24, 1860, reprinted in *Collected Works of Abraham Lincoln*, v. 4, p. 120. Rutgers University Press (1953,1990).

*P*ARLIAMENTARY PROCEDURES

He had no desire, he could assure gentlemen, ever to be out of order— though he never could keep long *in* order.

> "Remarks in United States House of Representatives Concerning Postal Contracts," January 5, 1848, reprinted in *Collected Works of Abraham Lincoln*, v. 1, p. 423. Rutgers University Press (1953, 1990).

*P*ASSION

Passion has helped us; but can do so no more. It will in future be our enemy. Reason, cold, calculating, unimpassioned reason, must furnish all the materials for our future support and defense.

"Lyceum Address," Springfield, Illinois, January 27, 1838, reprinted in *Collected Works of Abraham Lincoln*, v. 1, p. 115. Rutgers University Press (1953, 1990).

*P*ATRIOTISM

He loved his country partly because it was his own country, but mostly because it was a free country; and he burned with a zeal for its advancement, prosperity, and glory, because he saw in such the advancement, prosperity and glory of human liberty, human right, and human nature.

"Eulogy on Henry Clay," July 6, 1852, reprinted in *Collected Works of Abraham Lincoln*, v. 2, p. 126. Rutgers University Press (1953, 1990).

Clearly Lincoln's self-description.

Many free countries have lost their liberty; and *ours may* lose hers; but if she shall, be it my proudest plume, not that I was the *last* to desert, but that I *never* deserted her.

"Speech on the Sub-Treasury," December 26, 1839, reprinted in *Collected Works of Abraham Lincoln*, v. 1, p. 178. Rutgers University Press (1953, 1990).

The dogmas of the quiet past are inadequate to the stormy present. The occasion is piled high with difficulty, and we must rise with the occasion. As our case is new, so we must think anew, and act anew. We must disenthrall ourselves, and then we shall save our country.

"Annual Message to Congress," December 1, 1862, reprinted in *Collected Works of Abraham Lincoln*, v. 5, p. 537. Rutgers University Press (1953, 1990).

*P*AYMENT

He that dances should always pay the fiddler.

"Speech in Illinois Legislature Concerning the State Bank," January 11, 1837, reprinted in *Collected Works of Abraham Lincoln*, v. 1, p. 64. Rutgers University Press (1953, 1990).

The government cannot afford to accept services, and refuse payment for them.

Letter to Cary H. Fry, August 7, 1862, reprinted in *Collected Works of Abraham Lincoln*, v. 5, p. 360. Rutgers University Press (1953, 1990).

A poor widow, by the name of Baird, has a son in the Army, that for some offense has been sentenced to serve a long time without pay, or at most, with very little pay. I do not like this punishment of withholding pay—it falls so very hard upon poor families.

Letter to Edwin M. Stanton, March 1, 1864, reprinted in *Collected Works of Abraham Lincoln*, v. 7, p. 217. Rutgers University Press (1953, 1990).

*P*EACE

The man does not live who is more devoted to peace than I am. None who would do more to preserve it. But it may be necessary to put the foot down firmly.

"Address to the New Jersey General Assembly at Trenton, New Jersey," February 21, 1861, reprinted in *Collected Works of Abraham Lincoln*, v. 4, p. 237. Rutgers University Press (1953, 1990).

Engaged, as I am, in a great war, I fear it will be difficult for the world to understand how fully I appreciate the principles of peace. . . .

Letter to Samuel B. Tobey, March 19, 1862, reprinted in *Collected Works of Abraham Lincoln*, v. 5, p. 165. Rutgers University Press (1953, 1990).

Much is being said about peace; and no man desires peace more ardently than I. Still I am yet unprepared to give up the Union for a peace which, so achieved, could not be of much duration.

Letter to Isaac M. Schermerhorn, September 12, 1864, reprinted in *Collected Works of Abraham Lincoln*, v. 8, p. 1. Rutgers University Press (1953, 1990).

To bind up the nation's wounds. . . .

"Second Inaugural Address," March 4, 1865, reprinted in *Collected Works of Abraham Lincoln*, v. 8, p. 332. Rutgers University Press (1953, 1990).

*P*EOPLE, *THE*

The best sort of principle at that—the principle of allowing the people to do as they please with their own business.

"Speech in U.S. House of Representatives on the Presidential Question," July 27, 1848, reprinted in *Collected Works of Abraham Lincoln*, v. 1, p. 504. Rutgers University Press (1953, 1990).

We hold the true Republican position. In leaving the people's business in their hands, we can not be wrong.

"Speech in U.S. House of Representatives on the Presidential Question," July 27, 1848, reprinted in *Collected Works of Abraham Lincoln*, v. 1, p. 507. Rutgers University Press (1953, 1990).

The people—the people—are the rightful masters of both congresses, and courts. . . .

"Notes for speeches at Columbus and Cincinnati, Ohio," [September 16-17, 1859], reprinted in *Collected Works of Abraham Lincoln*, v. 3, p. 435. Rutgers University Press (1953, 1990).

See also GOVERNMENT

I . . . look to the American people and to that God who has never forsaken them.

"Address to the Ohio Legislature," Columbus, Ohio, February 13, 1861, reprinted in *Collected Works of Abraham Lincoln*, v. 4, p. 204. Rutgers University Press (1953, 1990).

It is upon the brave hearts and strong arms of the people of the country that our reliance has been placed in support of free government and free institutions.

"Speech to the Twelfth Indiana Regiment," May 13, 1862, reprinted in *Collected Works of Abraham Lincoln*, v. 5, p. 213. Rutgers University Press (1953, 1990).

Of the people, by the people, for the people.

"Gettysburg Address," November 19, 1863, reprinted in *Collected Works of Abraham Lincoln*, v. 7, p. 23. Rutgers University Press (1953, 1990).

Common looking people are the best in the world: that is the reason the Lord makes so many of them.

Diary entry, December 24, 1863, in Diary of John Hay, manuscript. Brown University Libraries.

PERSPECTIVE

It was true, the question appeared in a different aspect to persons in consequence of a difference in the point from which they looked at it.

"Remarks in United States House of Representatives Concerning Admission of Wisconsin into the Union," May 11, 1848, reprinted in *Collected Works of Abraham Lincoln*, v. 1, p. 470. Rutgers University Press (1953, 1990).

PERSUASION

We should urge it *persuasively*, and not *menacingly*. . . .

Letter to Horace Greeley, March 24, 1862, reprinted in *Collected Works of Abraham Lincoln*, v. 5, p. 169. Rutgers University Press (1953, 1990).

Referring to emancipation.

PHILOSOPHY

Some of you will be successful, and such will need but little philosophy. . . .

"Address before the Wisconsin State Agricultural Society, Milwaukee, Wisconsin," September 30, 1859, reprinted in *Collected Works of Abraham Lincoln*, v. 3, p. 481. Rutgers University Press (1953, 1990).

PLYMOUTH PLANTATION

The work of the Plymouth emigrants was the glory of their age. While we reverence their memory, let us not forget how vastly greater is our opportunity.

Letter to Joseph H. Choate, December 19, 1864, reprinted in *Collected Works of Abraham Lincoln*, v. 8, p. 170. Rutgers University Press (1953, 1990).

POLITICAL CAMPAIGNING

I would rejoice to be spared the labor of a contest; but "being in" I shall go it thoroughly, and to the bottom.

Letter to Benjamin F. James, January 14, 1846, reprinted in *Collected Works of Abraham Lincoln*, v. 1, p. 354. Rutgers University Press (1953, 1990).

I think too much reliance is placed in noisy demonstrations—importing speakers from a distance and the like. They excite prejudice and close the avenues to sober reason.

Letter to Andrew McCallen, June 19, 1858, reprinted in *Collected Works of Abraham Lincoln*, v. 2, p. 469. Rutgers University Press (1953, 1990).

*P*OLITICAL *DEFEAT*

With other men, to be defeated, was to be forgotten; but to him, defeat was but a trifling incident, neither changing him, or the world's estimate of him.

"Eulogy on Henry Clay," July 6, 1852, reprinted in *Collected Works of Abraham Lincoln*, v. 2, p. 125. Rutgers University Press (1953, 1990).

See also POLITICS

The election is over, the session is ended, and I am *not* Senator. . . .

Letter to William H. Henderson, February 21, 1855, reprinted in *Collected Works of Abraham Lincoln*, v. 2, p. 306. Rutgers University Press (1953, 1990).

I am glad I made the late race. It gave me a hearing on the great and durable question of the age, which I could have had in no other way; and though I now sink out of view, and shall be forgotten, I believe I have made some marks which will tell for the cause of civil liberty long after I am gone.

Letter to Anson G. Henry, November 19, 1858, reprinted in *Collected Works of Abraham Lincoln*, v. 3, p. 339. Rutgers University Press (1953, 1990).

This and the following quotations refer to the senatorial election of 1858, in which Douglas defeated Lincoln.

I expect the result of the election went hard with you. So it did with me, too, perhaps not quite so hard as you may have supposed. I have an abiding faith that we shall beat them in the long run.

Letter to Alexander Sympson, December 12, 1858, reprinted in *Collected Works of Abraham Lincoln*, v. 3, p. 346. Rutgers University Press (1953, 1990).

You are "feeling like h-ll yet." Quit that. You will soon feel better. Another "blow-up" is coming; and we shall have fun again.

Letter to Charles H. Ray, November 20, 1858, reprinted in *Collected Works of Abraham Lincoln*, v. 3, p. 342. Rutgers University Press (1953, 1990).

Of course I would have preferred success; but failing in that, I have no
regrets. . . .

Letter to Salmon P. Chase, April 30, 1859, reprinted in *Collected Works of Abraham Lincoln*, v. 3, p. 378.
Rutgers University Press (1953, 1990).

See also FAILURE

*P*OLITICAL HACKS

I misread his history if it does not show him [Franklin Pierce, presidential
candidate and later president] to have had just sufficient capacity, and no
more, of setting his foot down in the track, as his partizan leader lifted his
out of it—and so trudging along in the party team without a single
original tho't or independent action.

"Speech to the Springfield Scott Club," August 26, 1852, reprinted in *Collected Works of Abraham
Lincoln*, v. 2, p. 147. Rutgers University Press (1953, 1990).

*P*OLITICAL PARTIES

Our democratic friends seem to be in great distress because they think our
candidate for the Presidency don't suit *us*.

"Speech in U.S. House of Representatives on the Presidential Question," July 27, 1848, reprinted in
Collected Works of Abraham Lincoln, v. 1, p. 501. Rutgers University Press (1953, 1990).

A free people, in times of peace and quiet—when pressed by no common
danger—naturally divide into parties.

"Eulogy on Henry Clay," July 6, 1852, reprinted in *Collected Works of Abraham Lincoln*, v. 2, p. 126.
Rutgers University Press (1953, 1990).

The man who is of neither party, is not—cannot be, of any consequence.

"Eulogy on Henry Clay," July 6, 1852, reprinted in *Collected Works of Abraham Lincoln*, v. 2, p. 126.
Rutgers University Press (1953, 1990).

There never was a party in the history of this country, and there
probably never will be, of sufficient strength to disturb the general peace
of the country.

"Seventh and Last Debate with Stephen A. Douglas at Alton, Illinois," October 15, 1858, reprinted in
Collected Works of Abraham Lincoln, v. 3, p. 310. Rutgers University Press (1953, 1990).

Interesting to note how completely the two [parties] have changed hands as
to the principle upon which they were originally supposed to be divided. . . .
I remember once being much amused at seeing two partially intoxicated
men engage in a fight with their great-coats on, which fight, after a long, and
rather harmless contest, ended in each having fought himself *out* of his own
coat, and *into* that of the other.

> Letter to Henry L. Pierce and Others, April 6, 1859, reprinted in *Collected Works of Abraham Lincoln*,
> v. 3, p. 375. Rutgers University Press (1953, 1990).

The democracy of to-day hold the *liberty* of one man to be absolutely
nothing, when in the conflict with another man's right of *property*.
Republicans, on the contrary, are for both the *man* and the *dollar*; but
in the case of conflict, the man *before* the dollar.

> Letter to Henry L. Pierce and Others, April 6, 1859, reprinted in *Collected Works of Abraham Lincoln*,
> v. 3, p. 375. Rutgers University Press (1953, 1990).

If a house was on fire there could be but two parties. One in favor of
putting out the fire. Another in favor of the house burning.

> "Second Speech at Leavenworth, Kansas," December 5, 1859, reprinted in *Collected Works of Abraham
> Lincoln*, v. 3, p. 503. Rutgers University Press (1953, 1990).

*P*OLITICAL PATRONAGE

They have seen in his [Stephen A. Douglas's] round, jolly, fruitful face, post
offices, land offices, marshalships, and cabinet appointments, chargeships
and foreign missions, bursting and sprouting out in wonderful exuberance
ready to be laid hold of by their greedy hands. . . . Nobody has ever
expected me to be President. In my poor, lean, lank face nobody has ever
seen that any cabbages were sprouting out.

> "Speech at Springfield, Illinois," July 17, 1858, reprinted in *Collected Works of Abraham Lincoln*, v. 2,
> p. 506. Rutgers University Press (1953, 1990).

*P*OLITICAL PLATFORMS

Take the present democratic platform, and it does not propose to do a
single thing. It is full of declarations as to what ought *not* to be done, but
names no one to be done.

> "Speech to the Springfield Scott Club," August 26, 1852, reprinted in *Collected Works of Abraham
> Lincoln*, v. 2, p. 152. Rutgers University Press (1953, 1990).

POLITICIANS

A set of men who have interests aside from the interests of the people, and who ... are, taken as a mass, at least one long step removed from honest men. I say this with the greater freedom because, being a politician myself, none can regard it as personal.

"Speech in the Illinois Legislature," January 11, 1837, reprinted in *Collected Works of Abraham Lincoln*, v. 1, p. 65. Rutgers University Press (1953, 1990).

Men of the speaking sort of talent.

Letter to William H. Herndon, June 22, 1848, reprinted in *Collected Works of Abraham Lincoln*, v. 1, p. 491. Rutgers University Press (1953, 1990).

By much dragging of chestnuts from the fire for others to eat, his [James Buchanan's] claws are burnt off to the gristle, and he is thrown aside as unfit for further use.

"Speech at a Republican Banquet, Chicago, Illinois," December 10, 1856, reprinted in *Collected Works of Abraham Lincoln*, v. 2, p. 384. Rutgers University Press (1953, 1990).

POLITICS

The meeting, in spite of my attempt to decline it, appointed me one of the delegates, so that in getting [Edward D.] Baker [Lincoln's rival] the nomination, I shall be "fixed" a good deal like a fellow who is made groomsman to the man what has cut him out, and is marrying his own dear "gal."

Letter to Joshua F. Speed, March 24, 1843, reprinted in *Collected Works of Abraham Lincoln*, v. 1, p. 319. Rutgers University Press (1953, 1990).

If you have any more old horses, trot them out; any more tails, just cock them, and come at us.

"Speech in U.S. House of Representatives on the Presidential Question," July 27, 1848, reprinted in *Collected Works of Abraham Lincoln*, v. 1, p. 509. Rutgers University Press (1953, 1990).

In the war of extermination now waging between him [Senator Douglas] and his old admirers, I say, devil take the hindmost—and the foremost.

"Speech in the U.S. House of Representatives on the Presidential Question," July 27, 1848, reprinted in *Collected Works of Abraham Lincoln*, v. 1, p. 508. Rutgers University Press (1953, 1990).

I have no objection to "fuse" with any body provided I can fuse on ground which I think is right. . . .

> Letter to Owen Lovejoy, August 11, 1855, reprinted in *Collected Works of Abraham Lincoln*, v. 2, p. 316. Rutgers University Press (1953, 1990).

Like boys who have set a bird-trap, they are watching to see if the birds are picking at the bait and likely to go under.

> "Fragment of a Speech," [c. May 18, 1858], reprinted in *Collected Works of Abraham Lincoln*, v. 2, p. 448. Rutgers University Press (1953, 1990).

These things *look* like the cautious *patting* and *petting* a spirited horse, preparatory to mounting him, when it is dreaded that he may give the rider a fall.

> "A House Divided," speech at Springfield, Illinois, June 16, 1858, reprinted in *Collected Works of Abraham Lincoln*, v. 2, p. 465. Rutgers University Press (1953, 1990).

But fight we must, and conquer we shall, in the end.

> Letter to Cyrus M. Allen, May 1, 1860, reprinted in *Collected Works of Abraham Lincoln*, v. 4, p. 46. Rutgers University Press (1953, 1990).
>
> On opposing slavery extension.

Unanimity is impossible.

> "First Inaugural Address," March 4, 1861, reprinted in *Collected Works of Abraham Lincoln*, v. 6, p. 350. Rutgers University Press (1953, 1990).

If both factions, or neither, shall abuse you, you will probably be about right. Beware of being assailed by one, and praised by the other.

> Letter to John M. Schofield, May 27, 1863, reprinted in *Collected Works of Abraham Lincoln*, v. 6, p. 234. Rutgers University Press (1953, 1990).

Do we gain anything by opening one leak to stop another? Do we gain anything by quieting one clamor, merely to open another, and probably a larger one?

> Letter to Alexander K. McClure, June 30, 1863, reprinted in *Collected Works of Abraham Lincoln*, v. 6, p. 311. Rutgers University Press (1953, 1990).

I am in favor of short statutes of limitations in politics.

> Entry for August 23, 1864, reprinted in *Diary of John Hay*, manuscript. Brown University Libraries.

As a general rule, I abstain from reading the reports of attacks upon myself, wishing not to be provoked by that to which I cannot properly offer an answer.

> "Last Public Address," April 11, 1865, reprinted in *Collected Works of Abraham Lincoln*, v. 8, p. 401. Rutgers University Press (1953, 1990).

POLITICS AND MONEY

I cannot enter the ring on the money basis—first, because, in the main, it is wrong; and secondly, I have not, and can not get, the money.

Letter to Mark W. Delahay, March 16, 1860, reprinted in *Collected Works of Abraham Lincoln*, v. 4, p. 32. Rutgers University Press (1953, 1990).

I say, in the main, the use of money is wrong; but for certain objects, in a political contest, the use of some is both right and indispensable.

Letter to Mark W. Delahay, March 16, 1860, reprinted in *Collected Works of Abraham Lincoln*, v. 4, p. 32. Rutgers University Press (1953, 1990).

The money part of the arrangement you propose is, with me, an impossibility. I could not raise ten thousand dollars if it would save me from the fate of John Brown. Nor have my friends, so far as I know, yet reached the point of staking any money on my chances of success.

Letter to E. Stafford, March 17, 1860, reprinted in *Collected Works of Abraham Lincoln*, v. 4, p. 33. Rutgers University Press (1953, 1990).

POLITICS AND WAR

In this time of national peril I would have preferred to meet you upon a level one step higher than any party platform; because I am sure that from such more elevated position, we could do better battle for the country we all love, than we possibly can from those lower ones, where from the force of habit, the prejudices of the past, and selfish hopes of the future, we are sure to expend much of our ingenuity and strength, in finding fault with, and aiming blows at each other.

Letter to Erastus Corning and Others, [June 12], 1863, reprinted in *Collected Works of Abraham Lincoln*, v. 6, p. 267. Rutgers University Press (1953, 1990).

POPULAR SOVEREIGNTY

To illustrate the case—Abraham Lincoln has a fine meadow, containing beautiful springs of water, and well fenced, which John Calhoun had agreed with Abraham (originally owning the land in common) should be his, and the agreement had been consummated in the most solemn manner, regarded by both as sacred. John Calhoun, however, in the course of time, had become owner of an extensive herd of cattle—the prairie grass had become dried up and there was no convenient water to be had. John Calhoun then looks with a longing eye on Lincoln's meadow, and goes to it and throws down the fences, and exposes it to the ravages of his starving and famishing cattle. "You rascal," says Lincoln, "what have you done? What do you do this for?" "Oh," replies Calhoun, "everything is right. I have taken down your fence; but nothing more. It is my true intent and meaning not to drive my cattle into your meadow, nor to exclude them therefrom, but to leave them perfectly free to form their own notions of the feed, and to direct their movements their own way!"

"Editorial on the Kansas-Nebraska Act," September 11, 1854, reprinted in *Collected Works of Abraham Lincoln*, v. 2, p. 230. Rutgers University Press (1953, 1990).

What is [Senator Stephen A. Douglas'] Popular Sovereignty? Is it the right of the people to have Slavery or not have it, as they see fit, in the territories? I will state—and I have an able man to watch me—my understanding is that Popular Sovereignty, as now applied to the question of Slavery, does allow the people of a Territory to have Slavery if they want to, but does not allow them *not* to have it if they *do not* want it.

"First Debate with Stephen A. Douglas at Ottawa, Illinois," August 21, 1858, reprinted in *Collected Works of Abraham Lincoln*, v. 3, p. 18. Rutgers University Press (1953, 1990).

Definition of genuine popular sovereignty, in the abstract, would be about this: that each man shall do precisely as he pleases with himself, and with all those things which exclusively concern him.

"Speech at Columbus, Ohio," September 16, 1859, reprinted in *Collected Works of Abraham Lincoln*, v. 3, p. 405. Rutgers University Press (1953, 1990).

*P*OPULATION

Population must increase rapidly—more rapidly than in former times—and ere long the most valuable of all arts will be the art of deriving a comfortable subsistence from the smallest area of soil.

"Address before the Wisconsin State Agricultural Society, Milwaukee, Wisconsin," September 30, 1859, reprinted in *Collected Works of Abraham Lincoln*, v. 3, p. 481. Rutgers University Press (1953, 1990).

POVERTY

It is bad to be poor. I shall go to the wall for bread and meat, if I neglect my business this year as well as last.

Letter to Hawkins Taylor, September 6, 1859, reprinted in *Collected Works of Abraham Lincoln*, v. 3, p. 400. Rutgers University Press (1953, 1990).

PRACTICALITY

As appears to me that question has not been, nor yet is, a practically material one, and that any discussion of it, while it thus remains practically immaterial, could have no effect other than the mischievous one of dividing our friends. . . . [The question is] good for nothing at all—a merely pernicious abstraction.

"Last Public Address," April 11, 1865, reprinted in *Collected Works of Abraham Lincoln*, v. 8, p. 403. Rutgers University Press (1953, 1990).

Whether the seceded states were legally in the Union. See also SECESSION

PRAYERS

The prayers of both could not be answered; that of neither has been answered fully. The Almighty has His own purposes.

"Second Inaugural Address," March 4, 1865, reprinted in *Collected Works of Abraham Lincoln*, v. 8, p. 332. Rutgers University Press (1953, 1990).

Refers to the two sides in the Civil War.

PRECEDENT

A measure made expedient by a war is no precedent for times of peace.

"Opinion on the Admission of West Virginia into the Union," December 31, 1862, reprinted in *Collected Works of Abraham Lincoln*, v. 6, p. 28. Rutgers University Press (1953, 1990).

PRESERVATION

We shall sooner have the fowl by hatching the egg than by smashing it.

"Last Public Address," April 11, 1865, reprinted in *Collected Works of Abraham Lincoln*, v. 8, p. 404. Rutgers University Press (1953, 1990).

Reconstructing the Union.

PRESIDENCY

Were I president, I should desire the legislation of the country to rest with Congress, uninfluenced by the executive in its origin or progress, and undisturbed by the veto unless in very special and clear cases.

Fragment: "What General Taylor Ought to Say," [March? 1848], reprinted in *Collected Works of Abraham Lincoln*, v. 1, p. 454. Rutgers University Press (1953, 1990).

See also LEADERSHIP

To throw the responsibility. . . is fixing for the President the unjust and ruinous character of being a mere man of straw. This must be arrested, or it will damn us all inevitably. . . . He must occasionally say, or seem to say, by the Eternal, "I take responsibility." Those phrases were the "Samson's locks" of Gen. [Andrew] Jackson, and we dare not disregard the lessons of experience.

Letter to John M. Clayton, July 28, 1849, reprinted in *Collected Works of Abraham Lincoln*, v. 2, p. 60. Rutgers University Press (1953, 1990).

The Presidency, even to the most experienced politicians, is no bed of roses. . . .

"Eulogy on Zachary Taylor," July 25, 1850, reprinted in *Collected Works of Abraham Lincoln*, v. 2, p. 89. Rutgers University Press (1953, 1990).

No human being can fill that station and escape censure.

"Eulogy on Zachary Taylor," July 25, 1850, reprinted in *Collected Works of Abraham Lincoln*, v. 2, p. 89. Rutgers University Press (1953, 1990).

If constitutionally we elect a President, and therefore you undertake to destroy the Union, it will be our duty to deal with you as old John Brown has been dealt with.

"Speech at Leavenworth, Kansas," December 3, 1859, reprinted in *Collected Works of Abraham Lincoln*, v. 3, p. 502. Rutgers University Press (1953, 1990).

Remembering that when not a very great man begins to be mentioned for a very great position, his head is very likely to be a little turned, I concluded I am not the fittest person to answer the questions you ask.

Letter to Richard M. Corwine, April 6, 1860, reprinted in *Collected Works of Abraham Lincoln*, v. 4, p. 36. Rutgers University Press (1953, 1990).

The taste *is* in my mouth a little; and this, no doubt, disqualifies me, to some extent, to form correct opinions.

Letter to Lyman Trumbull, April 29, 1860, reprinted in *Collected Works of Abraham Lincoln*, v. 4, p.45. Rutgers University Press (1953, 1990).

I have been selected to fill an important office for a brief period. . . .
Should my administration prove to be a very wicked one, or what is more
probable, a very foolish one, if you the PEOPLE are but true to yourselves
and to the Constitution, there is but little harm I can do, *thank God!*

"Remarks at Lawrenceburg, Indiana," February 12, 1861, reprinted in *Collected Works of Abraham Lincoln*, v. 4, p. 197. Rutgers University Press (1953, 1990).

I bring to the work an honest heart; I dare not tell you that I bring a head
sufficient for it.

"Reply to Governor Andrew J. Curtin at Harrisburg, Pennsylvania," February 22, 1861, reprinted in *Collected Works of Abraham Lincoln*, v. 4, p. 243. Rutgers University Press (1953, 1990).

I freely acknowledge myself the servant of the people. . . .

Letter to James C. Conkling, August 26, 1863, reprinted in *Collected Works of Abraham Lincoln*, v. 6, p. 407. Rutgers University Press (1953, 1990).

I wish to avoid both the substance and the appearance of dictation.

Letter to Thomas Cottman, December 15, 1863, reprinted in *Collected Works of Abraham Lincoln*, v. 7, p. 67. Rutgers University Press (1953, 1990).

I have not permitted myself, gentlemen, to conclude that I am the best man
in the country; but I am reminded, in this connection, of a story of an old
Dutch farmer, who remarked to a companion once that "it was not best to
swap horses when crossing streams."

"Reply to Delegation from the National Union League," June 9, 1864, reprinted in *Collected Works of Abraham Lincoln*, v. 7, p. 384. Rutgers University Press (1953, 1990).

On the possibility of his reelection.

*P*RINCIPLES

That our principle [freedom & equality], however baffled, or delayed,
will finally triumph, I do not permit myself to doubt. Men will pass
away—die—die, politically and naturally; but the principle will live, and
live forever.

"Notes for Speeches at Columbus and Cincinnati, Ohio," [September 16-17, 1859], reprinted in *Collected Works of Abraham Lincoln*, v. 3, p. 436. Rutgers University Press (1953, 1990).

If any of us allow ourselves to seek out minor or separate points on which
there may be difference of views as to policy and right . . . [that will] keep

us from uniting in action upon a great principle in a cause on which we all agree. . . .

"Speech at Chicago, Illinois," March 1, 1859, reprinted in *Collected Works of Abraham Lincoln*, v. 3, p. 366. Rutgers University Press (1953, 1990).

The only danger will be the temptation to lower the Republican Standards in order to gather recruits. In my judgement such a step would be a serious mistake—would open a gap through which more would pass *out* than pass *in*.

Letter to Mark W. Delahay, May 14, 1859, reprinted in *Collected Works of Abraham Lincoln*, v. 3, p. 379. Rutgers University Press (1953, 1990).

At every step we must be true to the main purpose.

"Notes for Speeches at Columbus and Cincinnati, Ohio," [September 16-17, 1859], reprinted in *Collected Works of Abraham Lincoln*, v. 3, p. 436. Rutgers University Press (1953, 1990).

It can be truly said of him that while he was personally ambitious, he bravely endured the obscurity which the unpopularity of his principle imposed, and never accepted official honors, until those honors were ready to admit his principles with him.

Letter to John H. Bryant, May 30, 1864, reprinted in *Collected Works of Abraham Lincoln*, v. 7, p. 366. Rutgers University Press (1953, 1990).

Lincoln expresses his admiration for Owen Lovejoy.

Important principles may, and must, be inflexible.

"Last Public Address," April 11, 1865, reprinted in *Collected Works of Abraham Lincoln*, v. 8, p. 405. Rutgers University Press (1953, 1990).

*P*RINTING

At length printing came. It gave ten thousand copies of any written matter, quite as cheaply as ten were given before; and consequently a thousand minds were brought into the field where there was but one before.

"Second Lectures on Discoveries and Inventions," [February 11, 1859], reprinted in *Collected Works of Abraham Lincoln*, v. 3, p. 362. Rutgers University Press (1953, 1990).

Printing . . . is but the *other* half—and in real utility, the *better* half—of writing; and that both together are but the assistants of speech in the communication of thoughts between man and man.

"Second Lecture on Discoveries and Inventions," [February 11, 1859], reprinted in *Collected Works of Abraham Lincoln*, v. 3, p. 362. Rutgers University Press (1953, 1990).

PROBLEMS

The smallest are often the most difficult things to deal with.

"Third Debate with Stephen A. Douglas at Jonesboro, Illinois," September 15, 1858, reprinted in *Collected Works of Abraham Lincoln*, v. 3, p. 135. Rutgers University Press (1953, 1990).

I would rather meet them *as* they come, than *before* they come, trusting that some of them may not come at all.

Letter to Hamilton R. Gamble, December 30, 1862, reprinted in *Collected Works of Abraham Lincoln*, v. 6, p. 23. Rutgers University Press (1953, 1990).

PROGRESS

Very much like stopping a skift [boat] in the middle of a river—if it was not going up, it *would* go down.

"Remarks in the Illinois Legislature," January 22–23, 1840, reprinted in *Collected Works of Abraham Lincoln*, v. 1, p. 196. Rutgers University Press (1953, 1990).

A new country is most favorable—almost necessary—to the emancipation of thought, and the consequent advancement of civilization and the arts.

"Second Lecture on Discoveries and Inventions," [February 11, 1859], reprinted in *Collected Works of Abraham Lincoln*, v. 3, p. 363. Rutgers University Press (1953, 1990).

See also CONSERVATISM

There are more mines above the Earth's surface than below it. All nature—the whole world, material, moral, and intellectual—is a mine. . . .

"Second Lecture on Discoveries and Inventions," [February 11, 1859], reprinted in *Collected Works of Abraham Lincoln*, v. 3, p. 358. Rutgers University Press (1953, 1990).

PROMISES

Judge Peters says I promised. I dont remember.

Memorandum: "Appointment of A. Keller, Jr.," [c. July? 1862], reprinted in *Collected Works of Abraham Lincoln*, v. 5, p. 296. Rutgers University Press (1953, 1990).

On appointment to West Point.

The world shall know that I will keep my faith to friends and enemies, come what will.

"Interview with Alexander W. Randall and Joseph T. Mills," August 19, 1864, reprinted in *Collected Works of Abraham Lincoln*, v. 7, p. 507. Rutgers University Press (1953, 1990).

Bad promises are better broken than kept. . . .

"Last Public Address," April 11, 1865, reprinted in *Collected Works of Abraham Lincoln*, v. 8, p. 402. Rutgers University Press (1953, 1990).

*P*ROMOTION

Please have the Adjutant General ascertain whether 2nd. Lieut. of Co. D. 2nd. Infantry—Alexander E. Drake, is not entitled to promotion. His wife thinks he is.

Letter to Simon Cameron, November 13, 1861, reprinted in *Collected Works of Abraham Lincoln*, v. 5, p. 22. Rutgers University Press (1953, 1990).

*P*ROPERTY

My faith in the proposition that each man should do precisely as he pleases with all which is exclusively his own, lies at the foundation of the sense of justice there is in me.

"Speech at Peoria, Illinois," October 16, 1854, reprinted in *Collected Works of Abraham Lincoln*, v. 2, p. 265. Rutgers University Press (1953, 1990).

See also CAPITAL; LABOR

I take it that it is best for all to leave each man free to acquire property as fast as he can. Some will get wealthy. I don't believe in a law to prevent a man from getting rich; it would do more harm than good.

"Speech at New Haven, Connecticut," March 6, 1860, reprinted in *Collected Works of Abraham Lincoln*, v. 4, p. 24. Rutgers University Press (1953, 1990).

Property is the fruit of labor—property is desirable—is a positive good in the world.

"Reply to New York Workingmen's Democratic Republican Association," March 21, 1864, reprinted in *Collected Works of Abraham Lincoln*, v. 7, p. 259. Rutgers University Press (1953, 1990).

That some should be rich, shows that others may become rich, and hence is just encouragement to industry and enterprise.

"Reply to New York Workingmen's Democratic Republican Association," March 21, 1864, reprinted in *Collected Works of Abraham Lincoln*, v. 7, p. 260. Rutgers University Press (1953, 1990).

Let not him who is houseless pull down the house of another; but let him labor diligently and build one for himself, thus by example assuring that his own shall be safe from violence when built.

"Reply to New York Workingmen's Democratic Republican Association," March 21, 1864, reprinted in *Collected Works of Abraham Lincoln*, v. 7, p. 260. Rutgers University Press (1953, 1990).

*P*ROSPERITY

He desired the prosperity of his countrymen partly because they were his countrymen, but chiefly to show to the world that freemen could be prosperous.

"Eulogy on Henry Clay," July 6, 1852 reprinted in *Collected Works of Abraham Lincoln*, v. 2, p. 126. Rutgers University Press (1953, 1990).

Sad evidence that, feeling prosperity, we forget right. . . .

"Speech at Peoria, Illinois," October 16, 1854, reprinted in *Collected Works of Abraham Lincoln*, v. 2, p. 274. Rutgers University Press (1953, 1990).

On pro-slavery arguments.

Let us hope . . . that by the best cultivation of the physical world, beneath and around us, and the intellectual and moral world within us, we shall secure an individual, social, and political prosperity and happiness, whose course shall be onward and upward, and which, while the earth endures, shall not pass away.

"Address before the Wisconsin State Agricultural Society, Milwaukee, Wisconsin," September 30, 1859, reprinted in *Collected Works of Abraham Lincoln*, v. 3, p. 482. Rutgers University Press (1953, 1990).

I wish all men to be free. I wish the material prosperity of the already free [extended to all] which I feel sure the extinction of slavery would bring.

Letter to Henry W. Hoffman, October 4, 1864, reprinted in *Collected Works of Abraham Lincoln*, v. 8, p.41. Rutgers University Press (1953, 1990).

Without the *Constitution* and the *Union*, we could not have attained the result; but even these are not the primary cause of our great prosperity.

There is something back of these, entwining itself more closely about the human heart. That something is the principle of "Liberty to all"—the principle that clears the *path* for all—gives *hope* to all—and, by consequence, *enterprise*, and *industry* to all.

"Fragment on the Constitution and Union," [c. January 1861?], reprinted in *Collected Works of Abraham Lincoln*, v. 4, p. 168. Rutgers University Press (1953, 1990).

See also AMERICAN DREAM; UNITED STATES

*P*ROSTITUTES

One of them . . . had a member of Congress in tow. He went home with her; and if I were to guess, I would say, he went away a somewhat altered man—most likely in his pockets, and in some other particular. The fellow looked conscious of guilt, although I believe he was unconscious that every body around knew who it was that had caught him.

Letter to Mary Todd Lincoln, July 2, 1848, reprinted in *Collected Works of Abraham Lincoln*, v. 1, p. 496. Rutgers University Press (1953, 1990).

*P*UBLIC OFFICE

There is nothing about me which would authorize me to think of a first class office; and a second class one would not compensate me for being snarled at by others who want it for themselves.

Letter to Joshua F. Speed, February 20, 1849, reprinted in *Collected Works of Abraham Lincoln*, v. 2, p. 28-29. Rutgers University Press (1953, 1990).

*P*UBLIC AND PRIVATE INTEREST

The public interest and my private interest have been perfectly parallel, because in no other way could I serve myself so well, as by truly serving the Union.

Letter to Isaac M. Schermerhorn, September 12, 1864, reprinted in *Collected Works of Abraham Lincoln*, v. 8, p. 1. Rutgers University Press (1953, 1990).

*P*UBLIC OPINION

A universal feeling, whether well or ill-founded, can not be safely disregarded.

"Speech at Peoria, Illinois," October 16, 1854, reprinted in *Collected Works of Abraham Lincoln*, v. 2, p. 256. Rutgers University Press (1953, 1990).

Our government rests in public opinion. Whoever can change public opinion can change the government. . . .

"Speech at a Republican Banquet in Chicago, Illinois," December 10, 1856, reprinted in *Collected Works of Abraham Lincoln*, v. 2, p. 385. Rutgers University Press (1953, 1990).

Public sentiment is everything. With public sentiment, nothing can fail; without it nothing can succeed. Consequently he who molds public sentiment goes deeper than he who enacts statutes or pronounces decisions.

"First Debate with Stephen A. Douglas at Ottawa, Illinois," August 21, 1858, reprinted in *Collected Works of Abraham Lincoln*, v. 3, p. 27. Rutgers University Press (1953, 1990).

Public opinion is founded, to a great extent, on a property basis. What lessens the value of property is opposed, what enhances its value is favored.

"Speech at Hartford, Connecticut," March 5, 1860, reprinted in *Collected Works of Abraham Lincoln*, v. 4, p. 9. Rutgers University Press (1953, 1990).

See also PROPERTY

*P*UBLIC WORKS

Let the nation take hold of the larger works, and the states the smaller ones; and thus, working in a meeting direction, discreetly but steadily and firmly, what is made unequal in one place may be equalized in another, extravagance avoided, and the whole country put on that career of prosperity, which shall correspond with its extent of territory, its natural resources, and the intelligence and enterprise of its people.

"Speech in United States House of Representatives on Internal Improvements," June 20, 1848, reprinted in *Collected Works of Abraham Lincoln*, v. 1, p. 490. Rutgers University Press (1953, 1990).

One man is offended because a road passes over his land, and another is offended because it does *not* pass over his. . . .

"Speech in United States House of Representatives on Internal Improvements," June 20, 1848, reprinted in *Collected Works of Abraham Lincoln*, v. 1, p. 488. Rutgers University Press (1953, 1990).

The improvements of this broad and goodly land, are a mighty interest. . . .

"Speech in United States House of Representatives on Internal Improvements," June 20, 1848, reprinted in *Collected Works of Abraham Lincoln*, v. 1, p. 488. Rutgers University Press (1953, 1990).

*P*UNISHMENT

I dismissed you as an example and a warning. . . . I bear you no ill will; and I regret that I could not have the example without wounding you personally.

Letter to John J. Key, November 24, 1862, reprinted in *Collected Works of Abraham Lincoln*, v. 5, p. 508. Rutgers University Press (1953, 1990).

*P*URPOSE AND EXPECTATION

Cannot the Judge [Senator Douglas] perceive the distinction between a *purpose* and an *expectation*. I have often expressed an expectation to die, but I have never expressed a *wish* to die.

"Speech at Springfield, Illinois," July 17, 1858, reprinted in *Collected Works of Abraham Lincoln*, v. 2, p. 514. Rutgers University Press (1953, 1990).

*Q*UAKERS

The Friends have had, and are having, a very great trial. On principle, and faith, opposed to both war and oppression, they can only practically oppose oppression by war. In this hard dilemma, some have chosen one horn and some the other.

Letter to Eliza P. Gurney, September 4, 1864, reprinted in *Collected Works of Abraham Lincoln*, v. 7, p. 535. Rutgers University Press (1953, 1990).

*Q*UARRELS

I am slow to listen to criminations among friends, and never espouse their quarrels on either side. My sincere wish is that both sides will allow bygones to be bygones, and look to the present and future only.

Letter to John M. Pomeroy, August 31, 1860, reprinted in *Collected Works of Abraham Lincoln*, v. 4, p. 103. Rutgers University Press (1953, 1990).

When I have friends who disagree with each other, I am very slow to take sides in their quarrel.

> Letter to Andrew G. Curtain, February 4, 1861, reprinted in *Collected Works of Abraham Lincoln*, v. 4, p. 184. Rutgers University Press (1953, 1990).

The advice of a father to his son "Beware of entrance to a quarrel, but being in, bear it that the opposed may beware of thee," is good, and yet not the best. Quarrel not at all. No man resolved to make the most of himself can spare time for personal contention. Still less can he afford to take all the consequences, including the vitiating of his temper, and the loss of self-control.

> Letter to James M. Cutts, Jr., October 26, 1863, reprinted in *Collected Works of Abraham Lincoln*, v. 6, p. 538. Rutgers University Press (1953, 1990).

Yield larger things to which you can show no more than equal right; and yield lesser ones, though clearly your own. Better give your path to a dog, than be bitten by him in contesting for the right. Even killing the dog would not cure the bite.

> Letter to James M. Cutts, Jr., October 26, 1863, reprinted in *Collected Works of Abraham Lincoln*, v. 6, p. 538. Rutgers University Press (1953, 1990).

QUESTIONS

You don't know what you are talking about, my friend. I am quite willing to answer any gentleman in the crowd who asks an *intelligent* question.

> "Speech at Chicago, Illinois," July 10, 1858, reprinted in *Collected Works of Abraham Lincoln*, v. 2, p. 490. Rutgers University Press (1953, 1990).
>
> In discussion of the pro-slavery constitution of Kansas.

QUOTATIONS

In his [Senator Douglas'] quotations . . . the extracts were taken in such a way, as I suppose, brings them within the definition of what is called garbling—taking portions of a speech which, when taken by themselves, do not present the entire sense of the speaker as expressed at the time.

> "Seventh and Last Debate with Stephen A. Douglas at Alton, Illinois," October 15, 1858, reprinted in *Collected Works of Abraham Lincoln*, v. 3, p. 300. Rutgers University Press (1953, 1990).

I will not say that [Senator Douglas] willfully misquotes, but he does fail to quote accurately.

"Speech at Springfield, Illinois," July 17, 1858, reprinted in *Collected Works of Abraham Lincoln*, v. 2, p. 512. Rutgers University Press (1953, 1990).

[Senator Douglas] has not made the quotation with accuracy, but justice to him requires me to say that it is sufficiently accurate not to change its sense.

"Speech at Columbus, Ohio," September 16, 1859, reprinted in *Collected Works of Abraham Lincoln*, v. 3, p. 406. Rutgers University Press (1953, 1990).

*R*ACE RELATIONS

Let us discard all this quibbling about this man and the other man—this race and that race and the other race being inferior, and therefore they must be placed in an inferior position. . . .

"Speech at Chicago, Illinois," July 10, 1858, reprinted in *Collected Works of Abraham Lincoln*, v. 2, p. 501. Rutgers University Press (1953, 1990).

What I would most desire would be the separation of the white and black races.

"Speech at Springfield, Illinois," July 17, 1858, reprinted in *Collected Works of Abraham Lincoln*, v. 2, p. 521. Rutgers University Press (1953, 1990).

Who shall say, "I am the superior, and you are the inferior?"

"Speech at Springfield, Illinois," July 17, 1858, reprinted in *Collected Works of Abraham Lincoln*, v. 2, p. 520. Rutgers University Press (1953, 1990).

It was a false logic that assumed because a man did not want a negro woman for a *slave,* he must needs want her for a *wife.*

"Speech at Beardstown, Illinois," August 12, 1858, reprinted in *Collected Works of Abraham Lincoln*, v. 2, p. 541. Rutgers University Press (1953, 1990).

"We hold these truths to be self evident: that all men are created equal; that they are endowed by their Creator with certain unalienable rights; that among these are life, liberty and the pursuit of happiness." This was their majestic interpretation of the economy of the Universe. This was their lofty, and wise, and noble understanding of the justice of the

Creator to His creatures. Yes . . . to *all* His creatures, to the whole great
family of man.

"Speech at Lewistown, Illinois," August 17, 1858, reprinted in *Collected Works of Abraham Lincoln*, v. 2,
p. 546. Rutgers University Press (1953, 1990).

There is no reason in the world why the negro is not entitled to all the
natural rights enumerated in the Declaration of Independence, the right to
life, liberty and the pursuit of happiness. I hold that he is as much entitled
to these as the white man. I agree with Judge [Senator] Douglas he is not
my equal in many respects—certainly not in color, perhaps not in moral or
intellectual endowment. But in the right to eat the bread, without leave of
anybody else, which his own hand earns, *he is my equal and the equal of
Judge Douglas, and the equal of every living man.*

"First Debate with Stephen A. Douglas at Ottawa, Illinois," August 21, 1858, reprinted in *Collected
Works of Abraham Lincoln*, v. 3, p. 16. Rutgers University Press (1953, 1990).

Shall we free them and make them politically and socially our equals?
My own feelings will not admit of this, and if they would the feelings of
the great mass of white people would not. Whether this accords with strict
justice or not is not the sole question. A universal feeling, whether well or
ill-founded, cannot safely be disregarded. We cannot then make them
our equals.

"Speech at Carlinville," Illinois, August 31, 1858, reprinted in *Collected Works of Abraham Lincoln*, v. 3,
p. 79. Rutgers University Press (1953, 1990).

I am not, nor ever have been in favor of bringing about in any way the
social and political equality of the white and black races. . . . I am not
nor ever have been in favor of making voters or jurors of negroes, nor of
qualifying them to hold office, nor to intermarry with white people; and
I will say in addition to this that there is a physical difference between the
white and black races which I believe will for ever forbid the two races
living together on terms of social and political equality. And inasmuch as
they cannot so live, while they do remain together there must be the
position of superior and inferior, and I as much as any other man am in
favor of having the superior assigned to the white race. . . . I do not propose
dwelling longer at this time on this subject.

"Fourth Debate with Stephen A. Douglas at Charleston, Illinois," September 18, 1858, reprinted in
Collected Works of Abraham Lincoln, v. 3, p. 145. Rutgers University Press (1953, 1990).

I have never seen to my knowledge a man, woman or child who was in favor of producing a perfect equality, social and political, between negroes and white men.

"Fourth Debate with Stephen A. Douglas at Charleston, Illinois," September 18, 1858, reprinted in *Collected Works of Abraham Lincoln*, v. 3, p. 146. Rutgers University Press (1953, 1990).

Negro equality! Fudge!! How long, in the government of a God great enough to make and maintain this Universe, shall there continue knaves to vend, and fools to gulp, so low a piece of demagougeism as this.

Fragments: "Notes for Speeches," c. September 1859, reprinted in *Collected Works of Abraham Lincoln*, v. 3, p. 399. Rutgers University Press (1953, 1990).

If it was like two wrecked seamen on a narrow plank, when each must push the other off or drown himself, I would push the negro off or a white man either, but it is not; the plank is large enough for both. This good earth is plenty broad enough for white man and negro both, and there is no need of either pushing the other off.

"Speech at New Haven, Connecticut," March 5, 1860, reprinted in *Collected Works of Abraham Lincoln*, v. 4, p. 20. Rutgers University Press (1953, 1990).

Every man, black, white or yellow, has a mouth to be fed and two hands with which to feed it—and that bread should be allowed to go to that mouth without controversy.

"Speech at Hartford, Connecticut," March 5, 1860, reprinted in *Collected Works of Abraham Lincoln*, v. 4, p. 9. Rutgers University Press (1953, 1990).

I am not ashamed to confess that twenty five years ago I was a hired laborer, mauling rails, at work on a flat-boat—just what might happen to any poor man's son. I want every man to have the chance—and I believe a black man is entitled to it—in which he *can* better his condition—when he may look forward and hope to be a hired laborer this year and the next, work for himself afterward, and finally to hire men to work for him! That is the true system.

"Speech at New Haven, Connecticut," March 6, 1860, reprinted in *Collected Works of Abraham Lincoln*, v. 4, p. 24. Rutgers University Press (1953, 1990).

I . . . should, as the principle, treat them [freed black people] precisely as I would treat the same number of free white people in the same relation and condition.

Letter to Alpheus Lewis, January 23, 1864, reprinted in *Collected Works of Abraham Lincoln*, v. 7, p. 145. Rutgers University Press (1953, 1990).

They [black voters] would probably help, in some trying time to come, to keep the jewel of liberty within the family of freedom.

> Letter to Michael Hahn, March 13, 1864, reprinted in *Collected Works of Abraham Lincoln*, v. 7, p. 243. Rutgers University Press (1953, 1990).

The President has received yours of yesterday, and is kindly paying attention to it. As it is my business to assist him whenever I can, I will thank you to inform me, for his use, whether you are either a white man or black one, because in either case, you can not be regarded as an entirely impartial judge. It may be that you belong to a third or fourth class of *yellow* or *red* men, in which case the impartiality of your judgment would be more apparent.

> Letter to John McMahon, August 6, 1864, reprinted in *Collected Works of Abraham Lincoln*, v. 7, p. 483. Rutgers University Press (1953, 1990).

> Lincoln's reply to the following telegram: "what is justice & what is truth . . . Equal Rights & Justice to all white men in the United States forever. White men is in class number one & black men is in class number two & must be governed by white men forever." Lincoln was enough of a politician to direct his secretary to send the reply under his own name. But Lincoln would not forego the pleasure of writing the rejoinder himself.

> See also BLACK PEOPLE DEGRADED; BLACK SOLDIERS; DECLARATION OF INDEPENDENCE; EMANCIPATION; SLAVERY

REACTIONARIES

Though they blazed, like tallow-candles for a century, at last they flickered in the socket, died out, stank in the dark for a brief season, and were remembered no more, even by the smell.

> Fragment on the "Struggle Against Slavery," [c. July 1858], reprinted in *Collected Works of Abraham Lincoln*, v. 2, p. 482. Rutgers University Press (1953, 1990).

> On supporters of slavery in Great Britain.

READING

A capacity, and taste, for reading, gives access to whatever has already been discovered by others. It is the key, or one of the keys, to the already solved problems.

> "Address before the Wisconsin State Agricultural Society, Milwaukee, Wisconsin," September 30, 1859, reprinted in *Collected Works of Abraham Lincoln*, v. 3, p. 480. Rutgers University Press (1953, 1990).

REASON AND AUTHORITY

There are two ways of establishing a proposition. One is by trying to demonstrate it upon reason; and the other is to show that great men in former times have thought so and so, and thus to pass it by the weight of pure authority.

"Speech at Columbus, Ohio," September 16, 1859, reprinted in *Collected Works of Abraham Lincoln*, v. 3, p. 416. Rutgers University Press (1953, 1990).

See also PASSION

RECOMMENDATIONS

He is not worth a damn.

Letter to John Stuart, February 14, 1839, reprinted in *Collected Works of Abraham Lincoln*, v. 1, p. 143. Rutgers University Press (1953, 1990).

About William L.D. Ewing, Illinois politician.

Lest you might receive a different impression, I wish to say I hold Judge Parks in very high estimation; believing him to be neither knave or fool, but decidedly the reverse of both. Now, as I have called names so freely, you will of course consider this confidential.

Letter to Jesse Olds Norton, February 16, 1855, reprinted in *Collected Works of Abraham Lincoln, Second Supplement 1848-1865*, v. 11, p.10. Rutgers University Press (1990).

He is true as steel and his judgement is very good.

Letter to James W. Sommers, June 25, 1858, reprinted in *Collected Works of Abraham Lincoln*, v. 2, p. 475. Rutgers University Press (1953, 1990).

Describing James B. McKinley, Illinois lawyer.

He was very servicable to us then and is very needy now. Can anything be found for him. . . . Please try.

Letter to Salmon P. Chase, April 11, 1861, reprinted in *Collected Works of Abraham Lincoln*, v. 4, p. 327. Rutgers University Press (1953, 1990).

On William W. Danehower, Chicago lawyer.

I think after all, but am not sure, that he is a drunken loafer.

Letter to F. S. Bougan, n.d., reprinted in *Collected Works of Abraham Lincoln*, v. 8, p. 420. Rutgers University Press (1953, 1990).

Describing an unidentified man to F. S. Bougan.

RECONSTRUCTION IN LOUISIANA

Broken eggs cannot be mended; but Louisiana has nothing to do now but to take her place in the Union as it was, barring the already broken eggs. The sooner she does so, the smaller will be the amount of that which is past mending.

Letter to August Belmont, July 31, 1862, reprinted in *Collected Works of Abraham Lincoln*, v. 5, p. 350. Rutgers University Press (1953, 1990).

RECREATION

Constituted as man is, he has positive need of occasional recreation. . . .

"Address before the Wisconsin State Agricultural Society, Milwaukee, Wisconsin," September 30, 1859, reprinted in *Collected Works of Abraham Lincoln*, v. 3, p. 472. Rutgers University Press (1953, 1990).

REFUSALS

The public interest does not admit of it.

Letter to William H. Seward and Salmon P. Chase, December 20, 1862, reprinted in *Collected Works of Abraham Lincoln*, v. 6, p.12. Rutgers University Press (1953, 1990).

Not accepting resignations of two leading cabinet members.

I think you do not know how embarrassing your request is [for permits to trade with enemy in cotton].

Letter to William Kellogg, June 29, 1863, reprinted in *Collected Works of Abraham Lincoln*, v. 6, p. 307. Rutgers University Press (1953, 1990).

The impropriety of bringing such cases to me is obvious to any one who will consider that I could not properly act on any case without understanding it, and that I have neither the means nor time, to obtain such understanding.

Letter to D. M. Leatherman, September 3, 1863, reprinted in *Collected Works of Abraham Lincoln*, v. 6, p. 431. Rutgers University Press (1953, 1990).

Overruling a decision about a property case in Memphis.

What nation do you desire Gen. Allen to be made Quarter-Master-General of? This nation already has a Quarter-Master-General.

Letter to Jesse K. Dubois and Ozias M. Hatch, September 15, 1863, reprinted in *Collected Works of Abraham Lincoln*, v. 6, p. 450. Rutgers University Press (1953, 1990).

To interfere under the circumstances would blacken my own character.

Letter to Samuel C. Pomeroy, November 8, 1863, reprinted in *Collected Works of Abraham Lincoln*, v. 7, p. 4. Rutgers University Press (1953, 1990).

Plea to pardon an evidently embezzling quartermaster.

Today I verbally told Colonel Worthington that I did not think him fit for a Colonel; and now, upon his *urgent* request, I put it in writing.

Memorandum, March 31, 1864, reprinted in *Collected Works of Abraham Lincoln*, v. 7, p. 276. Rutgers University Press (1953, 1990).

RELIGION

I do not think I could myself be brought to support a man for office whom I knew to be an open enemy of, and scoffer at, religion. Leaving the higher matter of eternal consequences, between him and his Maker, I still do not think any man has the right thus to insult the feelings, and injure the morals, of the community in which he may live.

"Handbill Replying to Charges of Infidelity," July 31, 1846, reprinted in *Collected Works of Abraham Lincoln*, v. 1, p. 382. Rutgers University Press (1953, 1990).

See also GOD

That I am not a member of any Christian Church, is true; but I have never denied the truth of the Scriptures; and I have never spoken with intentional disrespect of religion in general, or of any denomination of Christians in particular.

"Handbill Replying to Charges of Infidelity," July 31, 1846, reprinted in *Collected Works of Abraham Lincoln*, v. 1, p. 382. Rutgers University Press (1953, 1990).

I have often wished that I was a more devout man than I am.

"Remarks to Baltimore Presbyterian Synod," October 24, 1863, reprinted in *Collected Works of Abraham Lincoln*, v. 6, p. 535. Rutgers University Press (1953, 1990).

You say your husband is a religious man; tell him when you meet him, that I say I am not much of a judge of religion, but that, in my opinion, the religion that sets men to rebel and fight against their government, because, as they think, that government does not sufficiently help some men to eat their bread on the sweat of *other* men's faces, is not the sort of religion upon which people can get to heaven!

"Story written for Noah Brooks," December 6, 1864, reprinted in *Collected Works of Abraham Lincoln*, v. 8, p. 155. Rutgers University Press (1953, 1990).

REMEMBRANCE

We of this Congress and this administration will be remembered in spite of ourselves. No personal significance, or insignificance, can spare one or another of us.

"Annual Message to Congress," December 1, 1862, reprinted in *Collected Works of Abraham Lincoln*, v. 5, p. 537. Rutgers University Press (1953, 1990).

REPRIMANDS

Although what I am now to say is to be, in form, a reprimand, it is not intended to add a pang to what you have already suffered upon the subject to which it relates.

Letter to James M. Cutts, Jr., October 26, 1863, reprinted in *Collected Works of Abraham Lincoln*, v. 6, p. 538. Rutgers University Press (1953, 1990).

To a Peeping-Tom officer.

REPUBLICAN PARTY

The Republican star gradually rises higher everywhere.

Letter to Salmon P. Chase, April 30, 1859, reprinted in *Collected Works of Abraham Lincoln*, v. 3, p. 378. Rutgers University Press (1953, 1990).

RESIGNATIONS

O.H. Platt, trying to resign an office which he does not hold.

"Note on O.H. Platt," n.d., reprinted in *Collected Works of Abraham Lincoln*, v. 8, p. 425. Rutgers University Press (1953, 1990).

Your resignation of the office of Secretary of the Treasury, sent me yesterday, is accepted. Of all I have said in commendation of your ability and fidelity, I have nothing to unsay; and yet you and I have reached a point of mutual embarrassment in our official relation which seems can not be overcome, or longer sustained, consistently with the public service. Your Obt. Servt.

Letter to Salmon P. Chase, June 30, 1864, reprinted in *Collected Works of Abraham Lincoln*, v. 7, p. 419. Rutgers University Press (1953, 1990).

You have generously said to me more than once that whenever your resignation could be a relief to me, it was at my disposal. The time has come.

Letter to Montgomery Blair, September 23, 1864, reprinted in *Collected Works of Abraham Lincoln*, v. 8, p. 18. Rutgers University Press (1953, 1990).

RESPONSIBILITY

I am responsible . . . to the American people, to the Christian world, to history, and on my final account to God.

"Address at Sanitary Fair, Baltimore, Maryland," April 18, 1864, reprinted in *Collected Works of Abraham Lincoln*, v. 7, p. 302. Rutgers University Press (1953, 1990).

REVENGE

Blood can not restore blood, and government should not act for revenge. . . .

Letter to Edwin M. Stanton, May 17, 1864, reprinted in *Collected Works of Abraham Lincoln*, v. 7, p. 345. Rutgers University Press (1953, 1990).

See also MALICE

I wish you to do nothing merely for revenge, but that what you may do shall be solely done with reference to the security of the future.

Letter to General William S. Rosecrans, November 19, 1864, reprinted in *Collected Works of Abraham Lincoln*, v. 8, p. 116. Rutgers University Press (1953, 1990).

REVOLUTION

If the relative grandeur of revolutions shall be estimated by the great amount of human misery they alleviate, and the small amount they inflict, then, indeed, will this [temperance] be the grandest the world shall ever have seen.

"Temperance Address," February 22, 1842, reprinted in *Collected Works of Abraham Lincoln*, v. 1, p. 278. Rutgers University Press (1953, 1990).

Any people anywhere, being inclined and having the power, have the *right* to rise up, and shake off the existing government, and form a new one that suits them better.

Speech in United States House of Representatives: "The War with Mexico," January 12, 1848, reprinted in *Collected Works of Abraham Lincoln*, v. 1, p. 438. Rutgers University Press (1953, 1990).

It is a quality of revolutions not to go by *old* lines or *old* laws; but to break up both, and make new ones.

Speech in United States House of Representatives: "The War with Mexico," January 12, 1848, reprinted in *Collected Works of Abraham Lincoln*, v. 1, p. 439. Rutgers University Press (1953, 1990).

No oppressed people will *fight* and *endure* as our fathers did without the promise of something better than a mere change of masters.

"Fragment on the Constitution and the Union," [c. January? 1861], reprinted in *Collected Works of Abraham Lincoln*, v. 4, p. 169. Rutgers University Press (1953, 1990).

This country, with its institutions, belongs to the people who inhabit it. Whenever they shall grow weary of the existing government, they can exercise their *constitutional* right of amending it, or their *revolutionary* right to dismember, or overthrow it.

"First Inaugural Address," March 4, 1861, reprinted in *Collected Works of Abraham Lincoln*, v. 4, p. 269. Rutgers University Press (1953, 1990).

In considering the policy to be adopted for suppressing the insurrection, I have been anxious and careful that the inevitable conflict for this purpose shall not degenerate into a violent and remorseless revolutionary struggle.

"Annual Message to Congress," December 3, 1861, reprinted in *Collected Works of Abraham Lincoln*, v. 5, p. 48. Rutgers University Press (1953, 1990).

RIDICULE

I have not been much shocked by the newspaper comments. . . . Those comments constitute a fair specimen of what has occurred to me through life. I have endured a great deal of ridicule without much malice; and have received a great deal of kindness, not quite free from ridicule. I am used to it.

Letter to James H. Hackett, November 2, 1863, reprinted in *Collected Works of Abraham Lincoln*, v. 6, p. 559. Rutgers University Press (1953, 1990).

RIGHT AND WRONG

Stand with anybody that stands RIGHT. Stand with him while he is right and PART with him when he goes wrong.

"Speech at Peoria, Illinois," October 16, 1854, reprinted in *Collected Works of Abraham Lincoln*, v. 2, p. 273. Rutgers University Press (1953, 1990).

The eternal struggle between these two principles—right and wrong—throughout the world.

"Seventh and Last Debate with Stephen A. Douglas," October 15, 1858, reprinted in *Collected Works of Abraham Lincoln*, v. 3, p. 315 . Rutgers University Press (1953, 1990).

Groping for some middle ground between the right and wrong, vain as the search for a man who should be neither a living man nor a dead man. . . .

"Address at Cooper Institute," New York City, February 27, 1860, reprinted in *Collected Works of Abraham Lincoln*, v. 3, p. 550. Rutgers University Press (1953, 1990).

ROBBERS

He was very much in the position of the man who was attacked by a robber, demanding his money, when he answered, "my dear fellow, I have no money, but if you will go with me to the light, I will give you my note. . . ."

"Speech at Decatur, Illinois," February 22, 1856, reprinted in *Collected Works of Abraham Lincoln*, v. 2, p. 333. Rutgers University Press (1953, 1990).

SATISFACTION

In this troublesome world, we are never quite satisfied.

Letter to Mary Todd Lincoln, April 16, 1848, reprinted in *Collected Works of Abraham Lincoln*, v. 1, p. 465. Rutgers University Press (1953, 1990).

SECESSION

It is safe to assert that no government proper ever had a provision in its organic law for its own termination. Continue to execute all the express provisions of our national Constitution, and the Union will endure forever—it being impossible to destroy it, except by some action not provided for in the instrument itself.

"First Inaugural Address," March 4, 1861, reprinted in *Collected Works of Abraham Lincoln*, v. 4, p. 252. Rutgers University Press (1953, 1990).

Physically speaking, we cannot separate. We cannot remove our respective sections from each other, nor build an impassable wall between them. A husband and wife may be divorced, and go out of the presence, and beyond the reach of each other; but the different parts of our country cannot do this. They cannot but remain face to face; and intercourse, either amicable or hostile, must continue between them.

"First Inaugural Address," March 4, 1861, reprinted in *Collected Works of Abraham Lincoln*, v. 4, p. 259. Rutgers University Press (1953, 1990).

I have always thought the act of secession is legally nothing, and needs no repealing.

Letter to Benjamin F. Flanders, November 9, 1863, reprinted in *Collected Works of Abraham Lincoln*, v. 7, p. 6. Rutgers University Press (1953, 1990).

*S*ELF-DECEPTION

He does not attempt to deceive us. He affords us no excuse to deceive ourselves.

"Annual Message to Congress," December 6, 1864, reprinted in *Collected Works of Abraham Lincoln*, v. 8, p. 151. Rutgers University Press (1953, 1990).

On Confederate president Jefferson Davis.

*S*ELF-INCRIMINATION

Treat him with mercy as he makes the disclosure himself.

"Endorsement Concerning James W. Hughlett," November 7, 1864, reprinted in *Collected Works of Abraham Lincoln*, v. 8, p.94. Rutgers University Press (1953, 1990).

Comment on letter about a Maryland volunteer who drew undue pay.

*S*ELF-INTEREST

We have been mistaken all our lives if we do not know whites as well as blacks look to their self-interest.

"Address on Colonization to a Deputation of Negroes," August 14, 1862, reprinted in *Collected Works of Abraham Lincoln*, v. 5, p. 374. Rutgers University Press (1953, 1990).

SELF-RESPECT

It is difficult to make a man miserable while he feels worthy of himself, and claims kindred to the great God who made him.

"Address on Colonization to a Deputation of Negroes," August 14, 1862, reprinted in *Collected Works of Abraham Lincoln*, v. 5, p. 373. Rutgers University Press (1953, 1990).

SELFISHNESS

It looked so fiendishly selfish, so like throwing fathers and brothers overboard, to lighten the boat for our security. . . .

"Temperance Address," February 22, 1842, reprinted in *Collected Works of Abraham Lincoln*, v. 1, p. 275. Rutgers University Press (1953, 1990).

The Bible says somewhere that we are desperately selfish. I think we would have discovered that fact without the Bible.

"Seventh and Last Debate with Stephen A. Douglas at Alton, Illinois," October 15, 1858, reprinted in *Collected Works of Abraham Lincoln*, v. 3, p. 310. Rutgers University Press (1953, 1990).

See also GREED

SHAKESPEARE

I think nothing equals Macbeth. It is wonderful. Unlike you gentlemen of the [acting] profession, I think the soliloquy in Hamlet commencing "O, my offence is rank" surpasses that commencing "To be, or not to be." But pardon this small attempt at criticism.

Letter to James H. Hackett, August 17, 1863, reprinted in *Collected Works of Abraham Lincoln*, v. 6, p. 392. Rutgers University Press (1953, 1990).

The best compliment I can pay is to say, as I truly can, I am very anxious to see it again [*Falstaff*] played by actor James H. Hackett.

Letter to James H. Hackett, August 17, 1863, reprinted in *Collected Works of Abraham Lincoln*, v. 6, p. 392. Rutgers University Press (1953, 1990).

SILENCE

I am rather inclined to silence, and whether that be wise or not, it is at least more unusual nowadays to find a man who can hold his tongue than to find one who cannot.

"Remarks at the Monogahela House," Pittsburgh, Pennsylvania, February 14, 1861, reprinted in *Collected Works of Abraham Lincoln*, v. 4, p. 208. Rutgers University Press (1953, 1990).

SLAVERY

The institution of slavery is founded on both injustice and bad policy. . . .

"Protest in the Illinois Legislature on Slavery," March 3, 1837, reprinted in *Collected Works of Abraham Lincoln*, v. 1, p. 75. Rutgers University Press (1953, 1990).

Pharaoh's country was cursed with plagues, and his hosts were drowned in the Red Sea for striving to retain a captive people who had already served them more than four hundred years. May like disasters never befall us!

"Eulogy on Henry Clay," July 6, 1852, reprinted in *Collected Works of Abraham Lincoln*, v. 2, p. 132. Rutgers University Press (1953, 1990).

If A. can prove, however conclusively, that he may, of right, enslave B.— why may not B. snatch the same argument, and prove equally, that he may enslave A?—

You say A. is white, and B. is black. It is *color*, then; the lighter, having the right to enslave the darker? Take care. By this rule, you are to be slave to the first man you meet, with a fairer skin than your own.

You do not mean *color* exactly?—You mean the whites are *intellectually* the superiors of the blacks, and, therefore have the right to enslave them? Take care again. By this rule, you are to be slave to the first man you meet, with an intellect superior to your own.

But, say you, it is a question of *interest*; and, if you can make it your *interest*, you have the right to enslave another. Very well. And if he can make it his interest, he has the right to enslave you.

"Fragment on Slavery," [July 1, 1854?], reprinted in *Collected Works of Abraham Lincoln*, v. 2, p. 222. Rutgers University Press (1953, 1990).

The ant, who has toiled and dragged a crumb to his nest, will furiously defend the fruit of his labor, against whatever robber assails him. So plain, that the most dumb and stupid slave that ever toiled for a master, does constantly *know* that he is wronged. So plain that no one, high or low, ever does mistake it, except in a plainly *selfish* way; for although volume upon volume is written to prove slavery a very good thing, we never hear of the man who wishes to take the good of it, *by being a slave himself.*

"Fragment on Slavery," [July 1, 1854?], reprinted in *Collected Works of Abraham Lincoln*, v. 2, p. 222. Rutgers University Press (1953, 1990).

We were proclaiming ourselves political hypocrites before the world, by thus fostering Human Slavery and proclaiming ourselves, at the same time, the sole friends of Human Freedom.

"Speech at Springfield, Illinois," October 4, 1854, reprinted in *Collected Works of Abraham Lincoln*, v. 2, p. 242. Rutgers University Press (1953, 1990).

Our Republican robe is soiled, and trailed in the dust. Let us repurify it. Let us turn and wash it white, in the spirit, if not the blood, of the Revolution. . . . Let north and south—let all Americans—let all lovers of liberty everywhere—join in the great and good work. If we do this, we shall not only have saved the Union; but we shall have so saved it, as to make, and to keep it, forever worthy of the saving. We shall have so saved it, that the succeeding millions of free happy people, the world over, shall rise up, and call us blessed, to the latest generations.

"Speech at Peoria, Illinois," October 16, 1854, reprinted in *Collected Works of Abraham Lincoln*, v. 2, p. 276. Rutgers University Press (1953, 1990).

Slavery is founded in the selfishness of man's nature—opposition to it is [in?] his love of justice.

"Speech at Peoria, Illinois," October 16, 1854, reprinted in *Collected Works of Abraham Lincoln*, v. 2, p. 271. Rutgers University Press (1953, 1990).

The thing is hid away, in the constitution, just as an afflicted man hides away a wen or a cancer, which he dares not cut out at once, lest he bleed to death; with the promise, nevertheless, that the cutting may begin at the end of a given time.

"Speech at Peoria, Illinois," October 16, 1854, reprinted in *Collected Works of Abraham Lincoln*, v. 2, p. 274. Rutgers University Press (1953, 1990).

This *declared* indifference, but as I must think, covert *real* zeal for the spread of slavery, I can not but hate. I hate it because of the monstrous injustice of slavery itself. I hate it because it deprives our Republican example of its just influence in the world—enables the enemies of free institutions, with plausibility, to taunt us as hypocrites—causes the real friends of freedom to doubt our sincerity, and especially because it forces so many really good men amongst ourselves into an open war with the very fundamental principles of civil liberty—criticizing the Declaration of Independence, and insisting that there is no right principle of action but *self-interest.*

"Speech at Peoria, Illinois," October 16, 1854, reprinted in *Collected Works of Abraham Lincoln*, v. 2, p. 255. Rutgers University Press (1953, 1990).

I hate to see the poor creatures hunted down, and caught, and carried back to their stripes, and unrewarded toils; but I bite my lip and keep quiet.

Letter to Joshua F. Speed, August 24, 1855, reprinted in *Collected Works of Abraham Lincoln*, v. 2, p. 320. Rutgers University Press (1953, 1990).

It is hardly fair for you to assume, that I have no interest in a thing which has, and continually exercises, the power of making me miserable.

Letter to Joshua F. Speed, August 24, 1855, reprinted in *Collected Works of Abraham Lincoln*, v. 2, p. 320. Rutgers University Press (1953, 1990).

And then, the negro being doomed, and damned, and forgotten, to everlasting bondage, is the white man quite certain that the tyrant demon will not turn upon him too?

Fragment: "Notes for Speeches," [c. August 21, 1858], reprinted in *Collected Works of Abraham Lincoln*, v. 2, p. 553. Rutgers University Press (1953, 1990).

The one is the common right of humanity and the other the divine right of kings. It is the same principle in whatever shape it develops itself. It is the same spirit that says, "You work and toil and earn bread, and I'll eat it." No matter in what shape it comes, whether from the mouth of a king who seeks to bestride the people of his own nation and live by the fruit of their labor, or from one race of men as an apology for enslaving another race, it is the same tyrannical principle.

"Seventh and Last Debate with Stephen A. Douglas at Alton, Illinois," October 15, 1858, reprinted in *Collected Works of Abraham Lincoln*, v. 3, p. 315. Rutgers University Press (1953, 1990).

This is a world of compensations; and he who would *be* no slave, must consent to *have* no slave. Those who deny freedom to others deserve it not for themselves and under a just God, can not long retain it.

Letter To Henry L. Pierce and Others, April 6, 1859, reprinted in *Collected Works of Abraham Lincoln*, v. 3, p. 376. Rutgers University Press (1953, 1990).

When a new territory is opened for settlement, the first man who goes into it may plant there a thing which, like the Canada thistle, or some other of those pests of the soil, cannot be dug out by the millions of men who will come thereafter. . . .

"Speech at Columbus, Ohio," September 16, 1859, reprinted in *Collected Works of Abraham Lincoln*, v. 3, p. 409. Rutgers University Press (1953, 1990).

On slavery expansion into the territories.

I hold if the Almighty had ever made a set of men that should do all the eating and none of the work, he would have made them with mouths only and no hands, and if he had ever made another class that he had intended should do all the work and none of the eating, he would have made them without mouths and with all hands.

"Speech at Cincinnati, Ohio"—Omitted Portion, September 17, 1859, reprinted in *Collected Works of Abraham Lincoln, Supplement 1832–1865*, v. 10, p. 44. Rutgers University Press (1953, 1990).

Our best and greatest men have greatly underestimated the size of this question. They have constantly brought forward small cures for great sores—plasters too small to cover the wound.

"Speech at New Haven, Connecticut," March 5, 1860, reprinted in *Collected Works of Abraham Lincoln*, v. 4, p. 15. Rutgers University Press (1953, 1990).

Whether the owners of this species of property do really see it as it is, it is not for me to say, but if they do, they see it as it is through 2,000,000,000 of dollars, and that is a pretty thick coating.

"Speech at New Haven, Connecticut," March 5, 1860, reprinted in *Collected Works of Abraham Lincoln*, v. 4, p. 16. Rutgers University Press (1953, 1990).

Without slavery the rebellion could never have existed; without slavery it could not continue.

"Annual Message to Congress," December 1, 1862, reprinted in *Collected Works of Abraham Lincoln*, v. 5, p. 530. Rutgers University Press (1953, 1990).

Those who shall have tasted actual freedom I believe can never be slaves, or quasi slaves again.

Letter to Stephen A. Hurlbut, July 31, 1863, reprinted in *Collected Works of Abraham Lincoln*, v. 6, p. 358. Rutgers University Press (1953, 1990).

African Slavery . . . a war upon the rights of all working people.

"Reply to New York Workingmen's Democratic Republican Association," March 21, 1864, reprinted in *Collected Works of Abraham Lincoln*, v. 7, p. 259. Rutgers University Press (1953, 1990).

I never knew a man who wished to be himself a slave. Consider if you know any *good* thing, that no man desires for himself.

"On Slavery," March 22, 1864, reprinted in *Collected Works of Abraham Lincoln*, v. 7, p. 260. Rutgers University Press (1953, 1990).

I have always thought that all men should be free; but if any should be slaves it should be first those who desire it for *themselves*, and secondly those who *desire* it for *others*. Whenever I hear any one arguing for slavery I feel a strong impulse to see it tried on him personally.

"Speech to One Hundred Fortieth Indiana Regiment," March 17, 1865, reprinted in *Collected Works of Abraham Lincoln*, v. 8, p. 361. Rutgers University Press (1953, 1990).

I am naturally anti-slavery. If slavery is not wrong, nothing is wrong. I can not remember when I did not so think, and feel.

Letter to Albert G. Hodges, April 4, 1864, reprinted in *Collected Works of Abraham Lincoln*, v. 7, p. 281. Rutgers University Press (1953, 1990).

It may seem strange that any men should dare to ask a just God's assistance in wringing their bread from the sweat of other men's faces; but let us judge not that we be not judged.

"Second Inaugural Address," March 4, 1865, reprinted in *Collected Works of Abraham Lincoln*, v. 8, p. 332. Rutgers University Press (1953, 1990).

If we shall suppose that American Slavery is one of those offenses which, in the providence of God, must needs come, but which, having continued through His appointed time, He now wills to remove, and that He gives to both North and South, this terrible war, as the woe due to those by whom the offence came, shall we discern therein any departure from those divine attributes which the believers in a Living God always ascribe to Him? Fondly do we hope—fervently do we pray—that this mighty scourge of war may speedily pass away. Yet, if God wills that it continue, until all the wealth piled by the bond-man's two hundred and fifty years of unrequited toil shall be sunk, and until every drop of blood drawn with the lash, shall be paid by another drawn with the sword, as was said three thousand years ago, so still it must be said "the judgments of the Lord, are true and righteous altogether."

"Second Inaugural Address," March 4, 1865, reprinted in *Collected Works of Abraham Lincoln*, v. 8, p. 333. Rutgers University Press (1953, 1990).

S*OLDIERS*

With us every soldier is a man of character and must be treated with more consideration than is customary in Europe.

> Letter to Agenor-Etienne de Gasparin, August 4, 1862, reprinted in *Collected Works of Abraham Lincoln*, v. 5, p. 355. Rutgers University Press (1953, 1990).

In my position I am environed with difficulties. Yet they are scarcely so great as the difficulties of those who, upon the battle field, are endeavoring to purchase with their blood and their lives the future happiness and prosperity of this country.

> "Reply to Serenade in Honor of Emancipation Proclamation," September 24, 1862, reprinted in *Collected Works of Abraham Lincoln*, v. 5, p. 438. Rutgers University Press (1953, 1990).

Men who, by fighting our battles, bear the chief burthen of saving our country.

> Letter to Montgomery Blair, July 24, 1863, reprinted in *Collected Works of Abraham Lincoln*, v. 6, p. 346. Rutgers University Press (1953, 1990).

For it has been said, all that a man hath will he give for his life; and while all contribute of their substance the soldier puts his life at stake, and often yields it up in his country's cause. The highest merit, then, is due to the soldier.

> "Remarks at Closing of Sanitary Fair," Washington, D.C., March 18, 1864, reprinted in *Collected Works of Abraham Lincoln*, v. 7, p. 254. Rutgers University Press (1953, 1990).

God bless the soldiers and seamen. . . .

> "Response to Serenade," October 19, 1864, reprinted in *Collected Works of Abraham Lincoln*, v. 8, p. 53. Rutgers University Press (1953, 1990).

To care for him who shall have borne the battle and for his widow and his orphan. . . .

> "Second Inaugural Address," March 4, 1865, reprinted in *Collected Works of Abraham Lincoln*, v. 8, p. 332. Rutgers University Press (1953, 1990).

The United States don't need the services of boys who disobey their parents.

> Letter to Gideon Welles, n.d., reprinted in *Collected Works of Abraham Lincoln*, v. 8, p. 427. Rutgers University Press (1953, 1990).
>
> On discharging underage soldier who volunteered without parental permission.

Sons

Since I began this letter a messenger came to tell me Bob [Lincoln's oldest son] was lost; but by the time I reached the house, his mother had found him and had him whipped—and by now very likely he is run away again.

Letter to Joshua F. Speed, October 22, 1846, reprinted in *Collected Works of Abraham Lincoln*, v. 1, p. 391. Rutgers University Press (1953, 1990).

Tell Tad [Lincoln's youngest son] the goats and father are very well— especially the goats.

Letter to Mary Todd Lincoln, April 28, 1864, reprinted in *Collected Works of Abraham Lincoln*, v. 7, p. 320. Rutgers University Press (1953, 1990).

Sorrow

In this sad world of ours, sorrow comes to all; and, to the young, it comes with bitterest agony, because it takes them unawares. The older have learned to ever expect it.

Letter to Fanny McCullough, December 23, 1862, reprinted in *Collected Works of Abraham Lincoln*, v. 6, p. 16. Rutgers University Press (1953, 1990).

Southerners

As I have not felt, so I have not expressed any harsh sentiment towards our Southern brethren. I have constantly declared, as I really believed, the only difference between them and us, is the difference of circumstances.

Fragment: "Last Speech of the Campaign at Springfield, Illinois," October 30, 1858, reprinted in *Collected Works of Abraham Lincoln*, v. 3, p. 334. Rutgers University Press (1953, 1990).

Special Pleading

Of course you expected to *gain* something by this [request to backdate commission]; but you should remember that precisely so much as you should gain by it others would lose by it. If the thing you sought had been exclusively ours, we would have given it cheerfully; but being the right of other men, we having a merely arbitrary power over it, the taking it from them and giving it to you, became a more delicate matter, and more deserving of consideration.

Letter to General William S. Rosecrans, March 17, 1863, reprinted in *Collected Works of Abraham Lincoln*, v. 6, p. 139. Rutgers University Press (1953, 1990).

*S*PEECHES

As to speech making, by way of getting the hang of the House [of Representatives] I made a little speech two or three days ago on a post-office question of no general interest. I find speaking here and elsewhere about the same thing. I was about as badly scared, and no worse, as I am when I speak in court.

Letter to William H. Herndon, January 8, 1848, reprinted in *Collected Works of Abraham Lincoln*, v. 1, p. 430. Rutgers University Press (1953, 1990).

Reading from speeches is a very tedious business, particularly for an old man that has to put on spectacles, and the more so if the man be so tall that he has to bend over to the light.

"Speech at Chicago, Illinois," July 10, 1858, reprinted in *Collected Works of Abraham Lincoln*, v. 2, p. 489. Rutgers University Press (1953, 1990).

The speech at New York . . . went off passably well and gave me no trouble whatever. The difficulty was to make nine others, before reading audiences who had already seen all my ideas in print.

Letter to Mary Todd Lincoln, March 4, 1860, reprinted in *Collected Works of Abraham Lincoln*, v. 3, p. 555. Rutgers University Press (1953, 1990).

And now, my friends, have I said enough? There appears to be a difference of opinion between you and me, and I feel called upon to insist upon deciding the question myself.

"Speech at the Astor House, New York City," February 19, 1861, reprinted in *Collected Works of Abraham Lincoln*, v. 4, p. 231. Rutgers University Press (1953, 1990).

I have said nothing but what I am willing to live by, and, in the pleasure of Almighty God, die by.

"Speech at Independence Hall, Philadelphia," February 22, 1861, reprinted in *Collected Works of Abraham Lincoln*, v. 4, p. 241. Rutgers University Press (1953, 1990).

I have made a great many poor speeches in my life, and I feel considerably relieved now to know that the dignity of the position in which I have been placed does not permit me to expose myself any longer.

"Remarks at a Review of New York Regiments," July 4, 1861, reprinted in *Collected Works of Abraham Lincoln*, v. 4, p. 441. Rutgers University Press (1953, 1990).

I believe I shall never be old enough to speak without embarrassment when I [don't] have anything to talk about.

"Response to a Serenade," December 6, 1864, reprinted in *Collected Works of Abraham Lincoln*, v. 8, p. 154. Rutgers University Press (1953, 1990).

*S*PEED

Please say to these gentlemen [army paymasters] that if they do not work quickly I will make quick work with them.

Letter to John A. Andrew, August 12, 1862, reprinted in *Collected Works of Abraham Lincoln*, v. 5, p. 367. Rutgers University Press (1953, 1990).

See also TIME

*S*TATISTICS

One of the gentlemen from South Carolina [Robert Barnwell Rhett] very much deprecates these statistics. He particularly objects, as I understand him, to counting all the pigs and chickens in the land. I do not perceive much force in the objection.

"Speech in United States House of Representatives on Internal Improvements," June 20, 1848, reprinted in *Collected Works of Abraham Lincoln*, v. 1, p. 489. Rutgers University Press (1953, 1990).

The point—the power to hurt—of all figures, consists in the *truthfulness* of their application.

"Speech in U. S. House of Representatives," July 27, 1848, reprinted in *Collected Works of Abraham Lincoln*, v. 1, p. 509. Rutgers University Press (1953, 1990).

*S*TRIKES

I am glad to know that there is a system of labor where the laborer can strike if he wants to! I would to God that such a system prevailed all over the world.

"Speech at Hartford, Connecticut," March 5, 1860, reprinted in *Collected Works of Abraham Lincoln*, v. 4, p. 7. Rutgers University Press (1953, 1990).

SUCCESS

But the game is caught; and I believe it is true, that with the catching, end the pleasures of the chase. This field of glory is harvested, and the crop is already appropriated.

"Lyceum Address," Springfield, Illinois, January 27, 1838, reprinted in *Collected Works of Abraham Lincoln*, v. 1, p. 113. Rutgers University Press (1953, 1990).

Always bear in mind that your own resolution to succeed is more important than any other one thing.

Letter to Isham Reavis, November 5, 1855, reprinted in *Collected Works of Abraham Lincoln*, v. 2, p. 327. Rutgers University Press (1953, 1990).

SUPERIORITY

You will never make much of a hand at whipping us. If we were fewer in numbers than you, I think that you could whip us; if we were equal it would likely be a drawn battle; but being inferior in numbers, you will make nothing by attempting to master us.

"Speech at Cincinnati, Ohio," September 17, 1859, reprinted in *Collected Works of Abraham Lincoln*, v. 3, p. 454. Rutgers University Press (1953, 1990).

On southern whites.

SUPREME COURT

I grant you that an unconstitutional act is not a law; but I do not ask and will not take your construction of the Constitution. The Supreme Court of the United States is the tribunal to decide such questions, and we will submit to its decisions. . . .

"Speech at Galena, Illinois," July 23, 1856, reprinted in *Collected Works of Abraham Lincoln*, v. 2, p. 355. Rutgers University Press (1953, 1990).

We think its decisions on Constitutional questions, when fully settled, should control, not only the particular cases decided, but the general policy

of the country, subject to be disturbed only by amendments of the
Constitution as provided in that instrument itself.

"Speech at Springfield, Illinois," June 26, 1857, reprinted in *Collected Works of Abraham Lincoln*, v. 3, p. 401. Rutgers University Press (1953, 1990).

If this important decision [on the Dred Scott case] had been made by the
unanimous concurrence of the judges, and without any apparent partisan
bias, and in accordance with legal public expectation, and with the steady
practice of the departments throughout our history, and had been in no
part based on assumed historical facts which are not really true; or if
wanting in some of these, it had been before the court more than once,
and had there been affirmed and re-affirmed through a course of years, it
then might be, perhaps would be, factious, nay, even revolutionary, to not
acquiesce in it as a precedent.

"Speech at Springfield, Illinois," June 26, 1857, reprinted in *Collected Works of Abraham Lincoln*, v. 4, p. 401. Rutgers University Press (1953, 1990).

Judicial decisions are of greater or less authority as precedents, according
to circumstances. That this should be so accords both with common sense
and the customary understanding of the legal profession.

"Speech at Springfield, Illinois," June 26, 1857, reprinted in *Collected Works of Abraham Lincoln*, v. 3, p. 401. Rutgers University Press (1953, 1990).

*T*ARIFF PROTECTION

We shall not be able to re-establish the policy, until the absence of it, shall
have demonstrated the necessity for it, in the minds of men heretofore
opposed to it.

Letter to Edward Wallace, October 11, 1859, reprinted in *Collected Works of Abraham Lincoln*, v. 3, p. 487. Rutgers University Press (1953, 1990).

*T*AXES

The objection to paying arises from the want of ability to pay.

"Communication to the People of Sangamo County," March 9, 1832, reprinted in *Collected Works of Abraham Lincoln*, v. 1, p. 5. Rutgers University Press (1953, 1990).

I go for all sharing the privileges of the government who assist in bearing its burthens.

> Letter to the Editor of the *Sangamo Journal*, June 13, 1836, reprinted in *Collected Works of Abraham Lincoln*, v. 1, p. 48. Rutgers University Press (1953, 1990).

The only question is as to sustaining the change [to higher taxes] before the people. I believe it can be sustained, because it does not increase the tax upon the *"many poor"* but upon the *"wealthy few"*. . . .

> Letter to William S. Wait, March 2, 1839, reprinted in *Collected Works of Abraham Lincoln*, v. 1, p. 148. Rutgers University Press (1953, 1990).

By the direct tax system, the land must be literally covered with assessors and collectors, going forth like swarms of Egyptian locusts, devouring every blade of grass and other green thing.

> "Campaign Circular from Whig Committee," March 4, 1843, reprinted in *Collected Works of Abraham Lincoln*, v. 1, p. 311. Rutgers University Press (1953, 1990).

Doubtless some of those who are to pay, and not to receive, will object.

> "Annual Message to Congress," December 1, 1862, reprinted in *Collected Works of Abraham Lincoln*, v. 5, p. 531. Rutgers University Press (1953, 1990).

A tax law, the principle of which is that each owner shall pay in proportion to the value of his property, will be a dead letter, if no one can be compelled to pay until it can be shown that every other one will pay in precisely the same proportion according to value; nay even, it will be a dead letter, if no one can be compelled to pay until it is certain that every other one will pay at all—even in unequal proportion.

> "Opinion on the Draft," [September 14?], 1863, reprinted in *Collected Works of Abraham Lincoln*, v. 6, p. 448. Rutgers University Press (1953, 1990).

TEN CANNOTS LINCOLN DID NOT WRITE

You cannot bring about prosperity by discouraging thrift.

You cannot help small men by tearing down big men.

You cannot strengthen the weak by weakening the strong.

You cannot lift the wage earner by pulling down the wage payer.

You cannot help the poor man by destroying the rich.

You cannot keep out of trouble by spending more than your income.

You cannot further the brotherhood of man by inciting class hatred.

You cannot establish security on borrowed money.

You cannot build character and courage by taking away men's initiative and independence.

You cannot help men permanently by doing for them what they could and should do for themselves.

> Ann Landers column, *The Gettysburg Times*, July 26, 1995.
>
> An often reproduced Lincoln apocrypha. Readers of this book can judge to what degree Lincoln's spirit is represented in these words that are not his. See also INTRODUCTION

THOUGHT

Intensity of thought . . . will some times wear the sweetest idea thread-bare and turn it to the bitterness of death.

> Letter to Joshua F. Speed, January 3, 1842, reprinted in *Collected Works of Abraham Lincoln*, v. 1, p. 265. Rutgers University Press (1953, 1990).

Mind, all conquering *mind*.

> "Temperance Address," February 22, 1842, reprinted in *Collected Works of Abraham Lincoln*, v. 1, p. 271. Rutgers University Press (1953, 1990).

TIME

A stitch in time may save nine in this matter.

> Letter to Mason Brayman About Law Suit, March 31, 1854, manuscript, Lincoln Legal Papers.
> A warning about a pending law suit.

Time is everything.

> Letter to Union Governors, July 3, 1862, reprinted in *Collected Works of Abraham Lincoln*, v. 5, p. 304. Rutgers University Press (1953, 1990).

TITLES

Suppose you do not prefix the "Hon." to the address on your letters to me any more. I like the letters very much, but I would rather they should not have that upon them.

Letter to Mary Todd Lincoln, April 16, 1848, reprinted in *Collected Works of Abraham Lincoln*, v. 1, p. 465. Rutgers University Press (1953, 1990).

TOM-FOOLERY

He said he was riding *bass-ackwards* on a *jass-ack*, through a *patton-cotch*, on a pair of *baddle-sags*, stuffed full of *binger-gred,* when the animal *steered* at a *scump*, and the *lirrup-steather* broke, and throwed him in the *forner* of the *kence* and broke his *pishing-fole.* He said he would not have minded it much, but he fell right in a great *tow-curd*; in fact he said it give him a right smart *sick* of *fitness*—he had the *molera-corbus* pretty bad. He said, about *bray dake* he come to himself, ran home, seized up a *stick* of *wood* and split the *axe* to make a light, rushed into the house, and found the *door* sick abed, and his *wife* standing open. But thank goodness she is getting right *hat* and *farty* again.

"Bass-Ackwards," n.d., reprinted in *Collected Works of Abraham Lincoln*, v. 8, p. 420. Rutgers University Press (1953, 1990).

TROUBLE

This may be a little troublesome, but I believe it will prevent a greater amount of trouble in future.

Letter to Isaac Gibson, February 26, 1851, reprinted in *Collected Works of Abraham Lincoln*, v. 2, p. 101. Rutgers University Press (1953, 1990).

In preparation for a lawsuit.

TRUTH

You are compelled to speak; and your only alternative is to tell the *truth* or tell a *lie.* I can not doubt which you would do.

Letter to William H. Herndon, February 1, 1848, reprinted in *Collected Works of Abraham Lincoln*, v. 1, p. 447. Rutgers University Press (1953, 1990).

On Lincoln's opposition to the war with Mexico.

I planted myself upon the truth, and the truth only, so, as far I knew it, or could be brought to know it.

"Speech at Springfield, Illinois, July 17, 1858," reprinted in *Collected Works of Abraham Lincoln*, v. 2, p. 512. Rutgers University Press (1953, 1990).

If Judge [Senator Stephen A.] Douglas shall assert that I do not believe what I say, then he affirms what he cannot know to be true, and falls within the condemnation of his own rule.

Fragment: "Notes for Speeches," [c. August 21, 1858], reprinted in *Collected Works of Abraham Lincoln*, v. 2, p. 550. Rutgers University Press (1953, 1990).

I mean to put a case no stronger than the truth will allow.

"Third Debate with Stephen A. Douglas at Jonesboro, Illinois," September 15, 1858, reprinted in *Collected Works of Abraham Lincoln*, v. 3, p. 126. Rutgers University Press (1953, 1990).

I would then like to know how it comes about, that when each piece of a story is true, the whole story turns out false?

"Fourth Debate with Stephen A. Douglas at Charleston, Illinois," September 18, 1858, reprinted in *Collected Works of Abraham Lincoln*, v. 3, p. 184. Rutgers University Press (1953, 1990).

Truth is generally the best vindication against slander.

Letter to Edwin M. Stanton, July 14, 1864, reprinted in *Collected Works of Abraham Lincoln*, v. 7, p. 440. Rutgers University Press (1953, 1990).

TYRANNY

Broken by it I too may be; bow to it I never will.

"Speech on the Sub-Treasury," December 26, 1839, reprinted in *Collected Works of Abraham Lincoln*, v. 1, p. 178. Rutgers University Press (1953, 1990).

It is kindly provided that of all those who come into the world, only a small percentage are natural tyrants.

"Speech at Peoria, Illinois," October 16, 1854, reprinted in *Collected Works of Abraham Lincoln*, v. 2, p. 264. Rutgers University Press (1953, 1990).

UNDERSTANDING

So hard is it to have a thing understood as it really is.

Letter to William H. Seward, June 28, 1862, reprinted in *Collected Works of Abraham Lincoln*, v. 5, p. 292. Rutgers University Press (1953, 1990).

Union

Much as I hate slavery, I would consent to the extension of it rather than
see the Union dissolved, just as I would consent to any GREAT evil, to
avoid a GREATER one.

"Speech at Peoria, Illinois," October 16, 1854, reprinted in *Collected Works of Abraham Lincoln*, v. 2,
p. 270. Rutgers University Press (1953, 1990).

I understand a ship to be made for the carrying and preservation of the
cargo, and so long as the ship can be saved, with the cargo, it should never
be abandoned. . . . So long, then, as it is possible that the prosperity and the
liberties of the people can be preserved in the Union, it shall be my
purpose at all times to preserve it.

"Reply to Mayor Fernando Wood at New York City," February 20, 1861, reprinted in *Collected Works of
Abraham Lincoln*, v. 4, p. 233. Rutgers University Press (1953, 1990).

We are not enemies, but friends. We must not be enemies. Though passion
may have strained, it must not break our bonds of affection. The mystic
chords of memory, stretching from every battle-field, and patriot grave,
to every living heart and hearthstone, all over this broad land, will yet swell
the chorus of the Union, when again touched, as surely they will be, by the
better angels of our nature.

"First Inaugural Address," March 4, 1861, reprinted in *Collected Works of Abraham Lincoln*, v. 4, p. 271.
Rutgers University Press (1953, 1990).

If there be those who would not save the Union, unless they could at the
same time *save* slavery, I do not agree with them. If there be those who
would not save the Union unless they could at the same time *destroy*
slavery, I do not agree with them. My paramount object in this struggle *is*
to save the Union, and is *not* either to save or to destroy slavery. If I could
save the Union without freeing *any* slave I would do it, and if I could save
it by freeing *all* the slaves I would do it; and if I could save it by freeing
some and leaving others alone I would also do that. What I do about
slavery, and the colored race, I do because I believe it helps to save the
Union; and what I forbear, I forbear because I do *not* believe it would
help to save the Union.

Letter to Horace Greeley, August 22, 1862, reprinted in *Collected Works of Abraham Lincoln*, v. 5, p. 388.
Rutgers University Press (1953, 1990).

The statement was less the annunciation of principle than the maneuvering of a politician who had already made up his mind to forge ahead with emancipation. This he did in a month. Here he addressed those northern multitudes who would support a war for the Union, but not a war for emanicipation.

UNITED STATES

In the great journal of things happening under the sun, we, the American People... find ourselves in the peaceful possession of the fairest portion of the earth.... We find ourselves under the government of a system of political institutions, conducing more essentially to the ends of civil and religious liberty, than any of which the history of former times tells us.

"Lyceum Address," Springfield, Illinois, January 27, 1838, reprinted in *Collected Works of Abraham Lincoln*, v. 1, p. 108. Rutgers University Press (1953, 1990).

"The noblest political system the world ever saw."

"Speech at Peoria, Illinois," October 16, 1854, reprinted in *Collected Works of Abraham Lincoln*, v. 2, p. 276. Rutgers University Press (1953, 1990).

Just now, in civilization, and the arts, the people of Asia are entirely behind those of Europe; those of the East of Europe behind those of the West of it; while we, here in America, *think* we discover, and invent, and improve, faster than any of them. *They* may think this is arrogance; but they can not deny that Russia has called on us to show her how to build steam-boats and railroads....

"Second Lecture on Discoveries and Inventions," February 11, 1859, reprinted in *Collected Works of Abraham Lincoln*, v. 3, p. 363. Rutgers University Press (1953, 1990).

This favored land.

"Speech at Buffalo, New York," February 16, 1861, reprinted in *Collected Works of Abraham Lincoln*, v. 4, p. 220. Rutgers University Press (1953, 1990).

A fair examination of history has seemed to authorize a belief that the past action and influences of the United States were generally regarded as having been beneficent towards mankind.

Letter to the Workingmen of Manchester, England, January 19, 1863, reprinted in *Collected Works of Abraham Lincoln*, v. 6, p. 64. Rutgers University Press (1953, 1990).

VICTORY: MILITARY

I can never forget, whilst I remember anything, that about the end of last year, and beginning of this, you gave us a hard earned victory which, had there been a defeat instead, the nation could scarcely have lived over.

Letter to General William S. Rosecrans, August 31, 1863, reprinted in *Collected Works of Abraham Lincoln*, v. 6, p. 424. Rutgers University Press (1953, 1990).

VICTORY: POLITICAL

Wise councils may *accelerate* or *mistakes delay* it, but sooner or later the victory is sure to come.

"A House Divided:" Speech at Springfield, Illinois, June 16, 1858, reprinted in *Collected Works of Abraham Lincoln*, v. 2, p. 469. Rutgers University Press (1953, 1990).

VOTING

Thanks to our good old constitution, and organization under it. . . . [The country] only needs that every right thinking man, shall go to the polls, and without fear or prejudice, *vote* as he *thinks*.

"Fragment of a Speech" [c. May 18, 1858], reprinted in *Collected Works of Abraham Lincoln*, v. 2, p. 454. Rutgers University Press (1953, 1990).

It is not the qualified voters, but the qualified voters *who choose to vote,* that constitute the political power of the state.

"Opinion on the Admission of West Virginia into the Union," December 31, 1862, reprinted in *Collected Works of Abraham Lincoln*, v. 6, p. 27. Rutgers University Press (1953, 1990).

See also BLACK VOTERS; ELECTIONS

WAR

A world less inclined to wars, and more devoted to the arts of peace, than heretofore.

"Address before the Wisconsin State Agricultural Society, Milwaukee, Wisconsin," September 30, 1859, reprinted in *Collected Works of Abraham Lincoln*, v. 3, p. 481. Rutgers University Press (1953, 1990).

Suppose you go to war, you cannot fight always; and when, after much loss on both sides, and no gain on either, you cease fighting, the identical old questions, as to terms of intercourse, are again upon you.

"First Inaugural Address," March 4, 1861, reprinted in *Collected Works of Abraham Lincoln*, v. 4, p. 259. Rutgers University Press (1953, 1990).

Teaching all the folly of being the beginners of a war.

"Message to Congress in Special Session," July 4, 1861, reprinted in *Collected Works of Abraham Lincoln*, v. 4, p. 439. Rutgers University Press (1953, 1990).

What would you do in my position? Would you drop the war where it is? Or, would you prosecute it in future, with elder-stalk squirts, charged with rose water?

Letter to Cuthbert Bullitt, July 28, 1862, reprinted in *Collected Works of Abraham Lincoln*, v. 5, p. 346. Rutgers University Press (1953, 1990).

I sincerely wish war was an easier and pleasanter business than it is; but it does not admit of holy-days.

Letter to Thomas H. Clay, October 8, 1862, reprinted in *Collected Works of Abraham Lincoln*, v. 5, p. 452. Rutgers University Press (1953, 1990).

The unreasoning, and uncharitable passions, prejudices, and jealousies incident to a great national trouble such as ours, and . . . the vast and long-enduring consequences, for weal or for woe, which are to result from the struggle. . . .

Letter to Alexander Reed, February 22, 1863, reprinted in *Collected Works of Abraham Lincoln*, v. 6, p. 114. Rutgers University Press (1953, 1990).

Armies, the world over, destroy enemies' property when they can not use it; and even destroy their own to keep it from the enemy. Civilized belligerents do all in their power to help themselves, or hurt the enemy, except a few things regarded as barbarous or cruel. Among the exceptions are the massacre of vanquished foes, and non-combatants, male and female.

Letter to James C. Conkling, August 26, 1863, reprinted in *Collected Works of Abraham Lincoln*, v. 6, p. 408. Rutgers University Press (1953, 1990).

Actual war coming, blood grows hot, and blood is spilled. Thought is forced from old channels into confusion. Deception breeds and thrives. Confidence dies, and universal suspicion reigns. Each man feels an impulse to kill his neighbor, lest he be first killed by him. Revenge and retaliation follow. And all this, as before said, may be among honest men only.

Letter to Charles D. Drake and Others, October 5, 1863, reprinted in *Collected Works of Abraham Lincoln*, v. 6, p. 500. Rutgers University Press (1953, 1990).

Every foul bird comes abroad, and every dirty reptile rises up. These add crime to confusion. . . . Murders for old grudges, and murders for pelf, proceed under any cloak that will best cover for the occasion.

Letter to Charles D. Drake and Others, October 5, 1863, reprinted in *Collected Works of Abraham Lincoln*, v. 6, p. 500. Rutgers University Press (1953, 1990).

War, at the best, is terrible, and this war of ours, in its magnitude and in its duration, is one of the most terrible. It has deranged business, totally in many localities, and partially in all localities. It has destroyed property, and ruined homes; it has produced a national debt and taxation unprecedented, at least in this country. It has carried mourning to almost every home, until it can almost be said that the "heavens are hung in black."

"Speech at Great Central Sanitary Fair, Philadelphia, Pennsylvania," June 16, 1864, reprinted in *Collected Works of Abraham Lincoln*, v. 7, p. 394. Rutgers University Press (1953, 1990).

See also CIVIL WAR

*W*AR DEAD

From these honored dead we take increased devotion to that cause for which they gave the last full measure of devotion. . . .

"Gettysburg Address," November 19, 1863, reprinted in *Collected Works of Abraham Lincoln*, v. 7, p.23. Rutgers University Press (1953, 1990).

Those who here gave their lives that that nation might live.

"Gettysburg Address," November 19, 1863, reprinted in *Collected Works of Abraham Lincoln*, v. 7, p. 23. Rutgers University Press (1953, 1990)

We here highly resolve that these dead shall not have died in vain. . . .

"Gettysburg Address,"November 19, 1863, reprinted in *Collected Works of Abraham Lincoln*, v. 7, p. 23. Rutgers University Press (1953, 1990).

WAR MAKING POWER

Allow the President to invade a neighboring nation, whenever *he* shall deem it necessary to repel an invasion . . . and you allow him to make war at pleasure.

Letter to William H. Herndon, February 15, 1848, reprinted in *Collected Works of Abraham Lincoln*, v. 1, p. 451. Rutgers University Press (1953, 1990).

Kings had always been involving and impoverishing their people in wars, pretending generally, if not always, that the good of the people was the object. This, our Convention understood to be the most oppressive of all Kingly oppressions; and they resolved to so frame the Constitution that *no one man* should hold the power of bringing this oppression upon us.

Letter to William H. Herndon, February 15, 1848, reprinted in *Collected Works of Abraham Lincoln*, v. 1, p. 451. Rutgers University Press (1953, 1990).

Under the constitution, Congress, and not the president, declares war.

"Speech to the Springfield Scott Club, August 26, 1852," reprinted in *Collected Works of Abraham Lincoln*, v. 2, p. 153. Rutgers University Press (1953, 1990).

WAR'S CAUSE

Both parties deprecated war; but one of them would *make* war rather than let the nation survive; and the other would *accept* war rather than let it perish. And the war came.

"Second Inaugural Address," March 4, 1865, reprinted in *Collected Works of Abraham Lincoln*, v. 8, p. 332. Rutgers University Press (1953, 1990).

WAR REPARATIONS

That those who make a causeless war should be compelled to pay the cost of it, is too obviously just, to be called in question.

Letter to the Senate and House of Representatives, July 17, 1862, reprinted in *Collected Works of Abraham Lincoln*, v. 5, p. 329. Rutgers University Press (1953, 1990).

WAR WITH MEXICO

The blood of this war, like the blood of Abel, is crying to Heaven against him [President James K. Polk].

Speech in United States House of Representatives: "The War with Mexico," January 12, 1848, reprinted in *Collected Works of Abraham Lincoln*, v. 1, p. 439. Rutgers University Press (1953, 1990).

When the war began, it was my opinion that all those who, because of knowing too *little*, or because of knowing too *much*, could not conscientiously approve the conduct of the President, in the beginning of it, should, nevertheless, as good citizens and patriots, remain silent on that point, at least till the war should be ended.

Speech in United States House of Representatives: "The War with Mexico," January 12, 1848, reprinted in *Collected Works of Abraham Lincoln*, v. 1, p. 432. Rutgers University Press (1953, 1990).

See also WAR

WARNINGS

This is not the taunt of enemies, but the warning of friends. Is it quite safe to disregard it...?

"Speech at Peoria, Illinois," October 16, 1854, reprinted in *Collected Works of Abraham Lincoln*, v. 2, p. 276. Rutgers University Press (1953, 1990).

Warning that the United States is losing the influence of its example in the world because of slavery.

WEALTH

All our energies should be exerted to bring ... wealth and population among us as speedily as possible.

"Report and Resolutions Introduced," January 17, 1839, reprinted in *Collected Works of Abraham Lincoln*, v. 1, p. 135. Rutgers University Press (1953, 1990).

See also PROPERTY

WEALTHY, THE

If, however, the wealthy should, regardless of the justness of the complaint, as men often are, when interest is involved in the question, complain [about taxes] . . . it is still to be remembered, that *they* are not sufficiently numerous to carry the elections.

Letter to William S. Wait, March 2, 1839, reprinted in *Collected Works of Abraham Lincoln*, v. 1, p. 148. Rutgers University Press (1953, 1990).

WEATHER FORECASTS

It seems to me Mr. Capen knows nothing about the weather, in advance. He told me three days ago that it would not rain again till the 30th of April or 1st of May. It is raining now and has been for ten hours.

"Memorandum Concerning Francis L. Capen's Weather Forecasts," April 28, 1863, reprinted in *Collected Works of Abraham Lincoln*, v. 6, p. 190. Rutgers University Press (1953, 1990).

WHITE HOUSE

I happen temporarily to occupy this big White House. I am a living witness that any one of your children may look to come here as my father's child has.

"Speech to One Hundred Sixty-Sixth Ohio Regiment," August 22, 1864, reprinted in *Collected Works of Abraham Lincoln*, v. 7, p. 512. Rutgers University Press (1953, 1990).

WILL

His will was indomitable; but this quality often secures to its owner nothing better than a character for useless obstinacy.

"Eulogy on Henry Clay," July 6, 1852, reprinted in *Collected Works of Abraham Lincoln*, v. 2, p. 125. Rutgers University Press (1953, 1990).

Will springs from the two elements of moral sense and self-interest.

"Speech at Springfield, Illinois," June 26, 1857, reprinted in *Collected Works of Abraham Lincoln*, v. 2, p. 409. Rutgers University Press (1953, 1990).

By all means, don't say "if I can"; say "I will."

Letter to John C. Bagby, September 6, 1858, reprinted in *Collected Works of Abraham Lincoln*, v. 3, p. 90. Rutgers University Press (1953, 1990).

WINNERS AND LOSERS

The victor shall soon be the vanquished, if he relax in his exertion; and that the vanquished this year, may be victor the next, in spite of all competition.

"Address before the Wisconsin State Agricultural Society, Milwaukee, Wisconsin," September 30, 1859, reprinted in *Collected Works of Abraham Lincoln*, v. 3, p. 481. Rutgers University Press (1953, 1990).

WOMEN

I go for admitting all whites to the right of suffrage, who pay taxes or bear arms, (by no means excluding females.)

Letter to Editor of the *Sangamo Journal*, June 13, 1836, reprinted in *Collected Works of Abraham Lincoln*, v. 1, p. 48. Rutgers University Press (1953, 1990).

Political platform.

Others have been made fools of by the girls; but this can never be with truth said of me. I most emphatically, in this instance, made a fool of myself.

Letter to Mrs. Orville H. Browning, April 1, 1838, reprinted in *Collected Works of Abraham Lincoln*, v. 1, p. 119. Rutgers University Press (1953, 1990).

On courting Mary Owens.

The truth is I have never corresponded much with ladies; and hence I postpone writing letters to them, as a business which I do not understand.

Letter to Mrs. M. J. Green, September 22, 1860, reprinted in *Collected Works of Abraham Lincoln*, v. 4, p. 118. Rutgers University Press (1953, 1990).

Our noble women . . . angel-ministering to the suffering soldiers. . . .

> Letter to Edward Everett, November 20, 1863, reprinted in *Collected Works of Abraham Lincoln*, v. 7, p. 24. Rutgers University Press (1953, 1990).

I have never studied the art of paying compliments to women; but I must say that if all that has been said by orators and poets since the creation of the world in praise of woman were applied to the women of America, it would not do them justice for their conduct during this war.

> "Remarks at Closing of Sanitary Fair, Washington, D.C.," March 18, 1864, reprinted in *Collected Works of Abraham Lincoln*, v. 7, p. 254. Rutgers University Press (1953, 1990).

This lady would be appointed Chaplain of the First Wisconsin Heavy Artillery, only that she is a woman. The President has not legally anything to do with such a question, but has no objection to her appointment.

> Letter to Edwin M. Stanton, November 10, 1864, reprinted in *Collected Works of Abraham Lincoln*, v. 8, p. 102. Rutgers University Press (1953, 1990).

WORK

Half finished work generally proves to be labor lost.

> "Communication to the People of Sangamo County," March 9, 1832, reprinted in *Collected Works of Abraham Lincoln*, v. 1, p. 5. Rutgers University Press (1953, 1990).

If you intend to go to work, there is no better place than right where you are; if you do not intend to go to work, you can not get along any where. Squirming & crawling about from place to place can do no good. . . . *Go to work* is the only cure for your case.

> Letter to John D. Johnston, November 4, 1851, reprinted in *Collected Works of Abraham Lincoln*, v. 2, p. 111. Rutgers University Press (1953, 1990).

Every blade of grass is a study; and to produce two, where there was but one, is both a profit and a pleasure.

> "Address before the Wisconsin State Agricultural Society, Milwaukee, Wisconsin," September 30, 1859, reprinted in *Collected Works of Abraham Lincoln*, v. 3, p. 480. Rutgers University Press (1953, 1990).

Every man is proud of what he does *well;* and no man is proud of what he does *not* do well. With the former, his heart is in his work; and he will do twice as much of it with less fatigue. The latter performs a little imperfectly, looks at it in disgust, turns from it, and imagines himself exceedingly tired.

"Address before the Wisconsin State Agricultural Society, Milwaukee, Wisconsin," September 30, 1859, reprinted in *Collected Works of Abraham Lincoln*, v. 3, p. 475. Rutgers University Press (1953, 1990).

Work, work, work, is the main thing.

Letter to John M. Brockman, September 25, 1860, reprinted in *Collected Works of Abraham Lincoln*, v. 4, p. 121. Rutgers University Press (1953, 1990).

The lady—bearer of this—says she has two sons who want to work. Set them at it, if possible. Wanting to work is so rare a merit, that it should be encouraged

Letter to George D. Ramsay, October 17, 1861, reprinted in *Collected Works of Abraham Lincoln*, v. 4, p. 556. Rutgers University Press (1953, 1990).

*W*RITING

Writing . . . is the great invention of the world.

"Second Lecture on Discoveries and Inventions," February 11, 1859, reprinted in *Collected Works of Abraham Lincoln*, v. 3, p. 360. Rutgers University Press (1953, 1990).

*Y*OUTH

The way for a young man to rise, is to improve himself every way he can, never suspecting that any body wishes to hinder him.

Letter to William H. Herndon, July 10, 1848, reprinted in *Collected Works of Abraham Lincoln*, v. 1, p. 497. Rutgers University Press (1953, 1990).

He has a great passion—a perfect rage—for the "*new*". . . . His horror is for all that is old, particularly "Old Fogy"; and if there be any thing old which he can endure, it is only old whiskey and old tobacco.

"Second Lecture on Discoveries and Inventions," February 11, 1859, reprinted in *Collected Works of Abraham Lincoln*, v. 3, p. 357. Rutgers University Press (1953, 1990).

We have all heard of Young America. He is the most *current* youth of the age. Some think him conceited, and arrogant; but has he not reason to entertain a rather extensive opinion of himself? Is he not the inventor and owner of the *present,* and sole hope of the *future?*

"Second Lecture on Discoveries and Inventions," February 11, 1859, reprinted in *Collected Works of Abraham Lincoln*, v. 3, p. 356. Rutgers University Press (1953, 1990).

Go it while you're young!

Letter to William H. Herndon, July 11, 1848, reprinted in *Collected Works of Abraham Lincoln*, v. 1, p. 499. Rutgers University Press (1953, 1990).

You and those of your age are to take charge of this country when we older ones shall have gone. . . .

Letter to Willie Smith, February 23, 1864, reprinted in *Collected Works of Abraham Lincoln*, v. 7, p. 202. Rutgers University Press (1953, 1990).

It was very difficult to say sensible things.

"Remarks at Opening of Patent Office Fair," February 22, 1864, reprinted in *Collected Works of Abraham Lincoln*, v. 8, p. 154. Rutgers University Press (1953, 1990).

BIBLIOGRAPHY

Balser, Roy P., Marion Dolores Pratt, and Lloyd A. Dunlap, eds. *The Collected Works of Abraham Lincoln*, 9 vols. 1953–55. *Supplements*, 1972, 1991.

Beveridge, Albert J. *Lincoln, 1809–1858*, 2 vols., 1928.

Boritt, Gabor S. *Lincoln and the Economics of the American Dream*, 1994.

——, ed. *Lincoln the War President: The Gettysburg Lectures*, 1992.

Burlingame, Michael. *The Inner World of Abraham Lincoln*, 1994.

Charnwood, Lord. *Abraham Lincoln: A Biography*, 1917.

Cox, LaWanda. *Lincoln and Black Freedom: A Study in Presidential Leadership*, 1981.

Current, Richard N. *The Lincoln Nobody Knows*, 1958.

Davis, Cullom B. et al. *The Law Practice of Abraham Lincoln*, CD-ROM forthcoming 1997.

Davis, Rodney O. and Douglas L. Wilson, eds. *Herndon's Informants: Letters, Interviews, and Statements about Abraham Lincoln*, 2 vols., forthcoming 1997.

Donald, David. *Lincoln Reconsidered*, 1961.

——. *Lincoln*, 1995.

Fehrenbacher, Don E. *Prelude to Greatness*, 1962.

——. *Lincoln in Text and Context*, 1987.

Fehrenbacher, Don E. and Virginia Fehrenbacher. *Recollected Words of Abraham Lincoln*, 1996.

Hamilton, Charles, and Lloyd Ostendorf. *Lincoln in Photographs: An Album of Every Known Pose*, 1985.

Hanchett, William B. *The Lincoln Murder Conspiracies*, 1983.

Herndon, William H. *Herndon's Life of Lincoln*, Paul M. Angle, ed., 1961.

Holzer, Harold. *Dear Mr. Lincoln: Letters to the President*, 1993.

——, Gabor S. Boritt, and Mark E. Neely, Jr. *The Lincoln Image: Abraham Lincoln and the Popular Print*, 1984.

The Journal of the Abraham Lincoln Association.

Kunhardt, Philip B., Jr., Philip B. Kunhardt III, and Peter W. Kunhardt. *Lincoln*, 1992.

Lincoln Herald.

Lincoln Lore.

Luthin, Reinhard H. *The Real Abraham Lincoln,* 1960.

McPherson, James M. *Abraham Lincoln and the Second Amercian Revolution,* 1991.

Mellon, James. *The Face of Lincoln,* 1979.

Miers, Earl Schenck et al., eds. *Lincoln Day by Day: A Chronology,* 3 vols., 1991.

Neely, Mark E., Jr. *The Abraham Lincoln Encyclopedia,* 1982.

——. *The Fate of Liberty: Abraham Lincoln and Civil Liberties,* 1991.

——. *The Last Best Hope of Earth: Abraham Lincoln and the Promise of America,* 1993.

Nicolay, John G. and John Hay. *Abraham Lincoln: A History,* 1890.

Paludan, Phillip. *The Presidency of Abraham Lincoln,* 1994.

Peterson, Merrill. *Lincoln in American Memory,* 1994.

Randall, James G. *Lincoln the President,* 4 vols. (vol. 4 completed by Richard N. Current), 1945–55.

Sandburg, Carl. *Abraham Lincoln: The Prairie Years and the War Years,* 6 vols. 1926–39.

Strozier, Charles B. *Lincoln's Quest for Union: Public and Private Meanings,* 1982.

Thomas, Benjamin P. *Abraham Lincoln: A Biography,* 1952.

Williams, T. Harry. *Lincoln and His Generals,* 1952.

Wills, Garry. *Lincoln at Gettysburg: The Words that Remade America,* 1992.

Wolf, William J. *The Almost Chosen People: A Study of the Religion of Abraham Lincoln,* 1959.